Mastering the Oracle
Belline

A Complete Guide

Serge Pirotte

Copyright © 2024, by Serge Pirotte

ISBN: 979-8-9898569-1-6

All rights reserved. No part of this book may be reproduced or utilized in any form or by any means, electronic or mechanical, including photocopying, recording, or by any information storage and retrieval systems, without permission in writing from the author.

This book is dedicated to my granddaughter Melanie, who is continuing the divination tradition after me.

Table of Contents

Foreword	9
Introduction	11
First Steps	**15**
Where do we Start	17
A Humanistic Cartomancy	27
A Closer Look at the Cards	**29**
The Composition of the Oracle	31
1 - Destiny	33
2 - The Man's Star	36
3 - The Woman's Star	36
The Blue Card	39
The Sun	42
4 - Nativity	44
5 - Success	47
6 - Elevation	50
7 - Honors	53
8 - Thought-Friendship	56
9 - Countryside-Health	59
10 - Gifts	62
The Moon	65
11 - Betrayal	67
12 - Departure	70
13 - Inconstancy	73
14 - Discovery	76
15 - Water	79
16 Penates	82
17 - Disease	85
Mercury	88

18 - Change	90
19 - Money	93
20 - Intelligence	96
21 - Theft - Loss	99
22 - Enterprises	102
23 - Traffic	105
24 - News	108
Venus	111
25 - Pleasures	113
26 - Peace	116
27 - Union	119
28 - Family	122
29 - Love	125
30 - The Table	128
31 - Passions	131
Mars	134
32 - Meanness	136
33 - Trial	139
34 - Despotism	142
35 - Enemies	145
36 - Negotiations	148
37 - Fire	151
38 - Accident	154
Jupiter	157
39 - Support	159
40 - Beauty	162
41 - Heritage	165
42 - Wisdom	168
43 - Fame	171
44 - Hazard	174
45 - Happiness	177
Saturn	180
46 - Misfortune	182

47 - Sterility	185
48 - Fatality	188
49 - Grace	191
50 - Ruin	194
51 - Delay	197
52 - Cloister	200

Reading the Cards	**203**
Introduction	205
The Question	206
Shuffling and Laying Out the Cards	210
Reversed Cards	213
The Advice Spread	215
The French Cross	219
The Classic French Cross	219
An Extended Version	226
The Snapshot Spread	232
One Question, One Card	237

Appendices	**241**
Keywords	243
Marcel Forget, aka Belline	246

Foreword

The first time I held a Lenormand Oracle in my hands was at one of TABI's Tarot Conferences. I marvelled at why this beautiful little set of cards was not better known in divinatory circles. You could count the number of books written in French and German about the Lenormand on the fingers of one hand and there were even fewer books available for English speakers like myself.

But look how this has changed in the past few years! The Lenormand deck has exploded into divination consciousness and now there are new decks and books being created in many languages all over the world.

The latest 'forgotten' deck that deserves a similar return to the divination mainstage is the subject of this book, the Oracle Belline.

When Serge Pirotte started making regular posts on his social channels using the Belline, people were entranced by this deck which many of us had never seen before. I was fascinated by the naïve but effective images and, most importantly, the on-point readings that Serge was crafting from them.

Curiosity about the Belline and how to work with it has grown steadily and has now reached the point where a reliable reference book is sorely needed. After following his regular Belline readings online and attending several of his workshops at various divination conferences, I am convinced that there is no-one better-placed to write that book than Serge Pirotte, the man who has single-handedly brought the deck back to people's attention.

I was delighted when Serge revealed that he was writing his Belline book and even more thrilled when I had the opportunity to be one of his first readers. In Mastering The

Oracle Belline we have an expert companion with years of experience to guide us through our adventure with the 52 cards and the planets that govern them. Serge explains how to interpret the cards in a variety of ways – as an asset, a problem, as advice, the evolution of a situation and as an outcome – all supremely important to grasp when you are just beginning to work with a new divination system. He even includes some of his favourite spreads to get you started.

Like the Lenormand, the Oracle Belline deserves a return to popularity amongst the world's cartomancers. With Serge and this book as its champions, the Belline's renaissance looks assured.

Enjoy your adventure!
Alison Cross

Introduction

I have a convoluted history with the oracle Belline.

But let me first introduce myself as it may be relevant to the way I approach esotericism in general, and my philosophy in writing this book. I have the chance to have lived on two different continents, I speak fluently two languages and I have been immersed into two different cultures. Being born in Belgium, I moved to the USA in the 1990s. That allowed me to be immersed in two very different cultures and esoteric traditions, and all these elements certainly shape the way I use the cards.

Effectively, when it comes to divination, French practitioners are quite different compared to the English-speaking ones. For instance, it is natural for French cartomancers to read tarot with majors only, something which would be the exception among English-speaking people. Most of the oracles used in these different parts of the world are also often different.

It is far from my intention to give a history lesson, but when it comes to esotericism, France has a rich history covering more than four centuries. It predates much of what could be called the English tradition, which basically started much later, mostly under the influence of the Golden Dawn, at the end of the 19th century. Speaking and understanding two languages gave me the chance to have access to a lot of publications and to discover many different tarots, oracles and divination systems. The oracle we are looking at in this book is a creation of the 19th century, coming directly from that French tradition.

Back to more practical matters, some experiences change our life forever, but sometimes we don't see immediately their results. I started using a Tarot de Marseille and a

Lenormand oracle later in life; I can admit now that divination was my midlife crisis. This was after having dealt professionally with computers, operating systems, and programming languages for over twenty years. Coming from that rational world, and also following some other personal events, I certainly needed to fill my life with some form of spirituality, and these cartomancy tools allowed me to ask myself some existential questions and try to find a response to them.

Anyway, I was immediately hooked by these cards, and a few decades later, I am still, more than ever. Over time, I have collected many tarots and oracle decks, and I bought the one we are discussing in this book, the oracle Belline, on a whim about fifteen years ago. I had to have it as it is the oracle the most used in the French world of cartomancy.

For a long time, I used it sporadically and it stayed quite a lot in my bookshelf. I was getting it out of its box from time to time but in the beginning my interest in it waned quickly. The problem was that I was reading the Tarot and Lenormand professionally, and I did not believe it would be useful to include another tool in my practice. As I was using the tarot for advice and Lenormand for divination, for a long time I did not see the need to use anything else.

So, I reserved the oracle Belline mostly for personal readings, and I was always impressed by its accuracy. To the point that a few years ago, I had to reconsider the relative importance of my tools and I started to have the urge to use the Belline more and more. As a result I started to look at these images differently. And the more I looked at them, the more these images so simple in appearance started to work on my subconscious.

It was a strange feeling. I remember when I was a beginner with the tarot and Lenormand, I started to learn

Introduction

the cards by rote memorization, my intuition starting to kick in later.

But not with the oracle Belline, it seemed that I did not need any instruction and these simple images started talking to me on a more intimate level. As a result I started to use them more and more, still on a personal level, without being public at first about it. I was just creating my experience with them and journaling my feelings and readings, a very important step to get a deeper connection and check how accurate our predictions are.

Later, I read two books and followed a course on this oracle, but they did not bring much, they simply confirmed what I was feeling intuitively. Since then, I have included them in my professional practice.

These days, I see the oracle Belline as the Swiss Army knife of divination, or as a middle ground between the tarot and Lenormand. I feel that they are better than tarot for prediction, and better than Lenormand for advice. If I had to keep only one deck, it would without any doubt be this one, as it can reply with precision to any kind of question I ask it.

About a year ago, I started to put all my notes and journals in order. I spent most of my time with a dictionary and a dictionary of symbols, starting to give a more formal aspect to my writings. This book is the result of my personal journey with these card, and what I learned with them, it is divided in three parts.

Part 1 will show you how you can start researching this wonderful oracle; what method you can use in to order to facilitate your learning process.

In Part 2, we will go through all the cards one by one and give a detailed interpretation. This section can of course be read from the beginning to the end, but it can also be used later as a reference, when you need to check some particular aspect of a card during a reading.

In Part 3, I will discuss how to read the cards and describe a few spreads.

I hope you will enjoy discovering this wonderful oracle as much as I did.

Coventry, Rhode Island
February 2024

Part 1
First Steps

Because you need to learn how to walk before running

Where do we Start

When beginning with a new oracle, tarot, or divination system, it is always difficult to determine where to start and how to proceed. I did teach many students over the years, and this chapter is the result of my experience with them. At the same time, I see many beginners in divination groups struggling for a long time. Not that they are not capable of learning, I have no doubt about their capabilities or intentions, the main problem is usually how they approach learning a new system.

The bigger problem, when starting, is that we always want to do too much, we literally want to run before we learn how to walk properly. Would you expect, for instance, a seven year old to read and understand Shakespeare?

Or to take another, maybe more realistic example. Let's suppose we want to learn a new language, and let's look at two different approaches. One student is spending all their time in books, trying to assimilate the grammar and vocabulary, and practicing with other students. The other one spends most of their time with locals, trying to speak with them rather than doing rote memorization and caring much about the theory. After a few months, which one do you think will speak better with natives of the language? The second one of course, because nothing beats having some practical experiences once you have a basic knowledge.

So, why do we act differently when learning to read the cards? I see multitudes of people spending their time in books, making sure they're learning the right definitions, and doing a little bit of practice with other beginners in Facebook groups. Well, that's not getting a real life experience.

So, how do you build a solid foundation?

The most important point is to begin slowly. There is no need to learn all 53 cards of the oracle to start reading for practice. You could start for instance with the three cards not having a planet, the Sun cards, and the Moon cards. That would be a total of 17 cards to learn first. Just go with the name, a few keywords, and look at the picture. There is no need to know more when you start. You start reading this way and learn at the same time what the cards mean to you when faced with practical questions.

Read on any subject, read on what you can check quickly. For instance, how your meeting at work will go tomorrow, your neighbor's situation, or fictional stuff like TV shows, etc. Practice, practice, and practice more, and always verify the results and where you might have gone wrong.

And when you start to have a good feedback, add the cards for one more planet, another series of seven cards.

Repeat the same process, until you can use comfortably the complete deck. It will still be time to complete your theoretical knowledge when you become acquainted with all the cards.

At the same time, try to avoid a few common pitfalls.

Don't be emotional.

This is how you lose control. Most of the time, when reading for a subject that we have at heart, like most readings we do for ourselves, we quickly become too emotional and read in the cards what we would like to see instead of what is really there. That's because we are too attached to the outcome.

Be objective.

A very similar thing to being emotional. When we have someone we're reading for in front of us, it is easy to start having sympathy for the person and hoping they will get a good outcome. Sometimes, in that case, a bad card does not look too bad to us and we emphasize good cards, we lose our objectivity, and we don't deliver a fair and accurate reading anymore.

Read all the cards.

All the cards on the table should be read, in the order prescribed by the spread you use. About the same amount of time should be spent with each card. It is very easy to acquire the tendency to skip or not say much about the cards we don't like. Never forget, if a card is present, that's for a reason, it should be part of the interpretation. Some cards might seem difficult to interpret is some contexts, that's normal when learning and practicing will help you get over this hurdle.

Use a method, know your spreads.

The more you practice the same spreads, the easier they will become. As a rule of thumb, every hour of learning should roughly be divided in 15 minutes of theory and 45 minutes of practice, trying to interpret your cards in different combinations and contexts. The more practical experiences you have, the more proficient you will feel.

Let's look in detail at a few important points.

Which deck to use.

Among the many modern alternatives we can find today of the oracle Belline, which one should we choose?

When I started reading cards, the choice was easy, there was only one version of the oracle Belline. It was made by the French company Grimaud, under the instructions of Marcel Belline, and their version conformed to the original oracle that the Mage Edmond created.

Recently, quite a few new versions have appeared, and some of them tried to stay close to the original, while others strayed and became very different. While I understand completely that not everybody likes the original version, using clones when learning can quickly become problematic.

First, this book, as well as all the others you will find on the oracle Belline, were written using the original as a reference. As a result, it is very difficult to find documentation for a particular deck, outside of the sparse information coming with it.

Second, all clones, and some more than others, will often have very different images, and even sometimes different names for the cards, making their symbolism very divergent from the original oracle. Once again, you will be on your own to try to understand these differences.

There is no problem using clones when you know enough about the oracle, but for the purpose of starting up and learning, I strongly advise you to use the original deck.

Pick one system.

When learning, consistency is extremely important. Especially today, with the internet and globally available bookstores, you might find yourself faced with many different resources, books, blogs, videos, etc.

The problem with this abundance of sources is that each author has a different view of the cards, and at the beginning of our divination journey hesitation and too many different interpretations will disrupt your learning process and your intuition. It is much better to decide early on, on one source and one set of meanings, and to use them consistently while learning. Getting a good, stable foundation will boost your trust in the cards and yourself.

If you mix meanings from different sources, you will always hesitate on which one to use when putting a few cards on the table, and that will hurt your interpretation. There is nothing worse when starting than being faced with multiple choices of definitions all the time. Unconsciously, you will always hesitate when interpreting a card, and as a result your readings will lack precision, up to the point where you will quickly start to lose confidence in yourself.

The best way to learn is to stick to one system until you have a better understanding of the oracle. Pick a book, or a blog, or any resource, and work with it until your have a strong enough base. Later, it will be time to expand and gradually add other sources to your knowledge, you will have acquired enough wisdom to extract from these sources what makes sense to you and add these element to what you already know. What you want is to build a solid foundation, then to gradually increase to it, in a controlled manner.

Stick to the question.

When doing divination, you should start with the axiom that your cards always respond to the question you asked. It is important in that regard to make sure your question is well defined and agreed upon with the querent. I always advise my students to write the question on a piece of paper, that way we can always go back to what was written when a point of contention happens.

Let's not forget either that in order to give meaningful information, as opposed to generalities that will move nobody, your questions should be precise and correctly define the context or domain in which the interpretation will happen. We will look in detail how to ask a question in Part 3 of this book.

But for the moment, just remember that a question should be clear, simple, and define the context in which you want your cards to be interpreted. If your question is about work, your cards will respond about work. Even if some cards are first about love, they should still be interpreted in the context of work.

That's what I mean by "sticking to the question". For example, a card like Amor or Union, in the context of work, will not hint about a love affair with a coworker, but will show for instance how passionate you are about your work. Never try to deviate from the context, if the question was well defined, the cards will respond to what was asked.

When you have built a solid foundation, putting your cards in different contexts will also allow you to expand your vocabulary and see how you can use your cards in different domains.

Especially at the beginning, keep you interpretations simple, go to the essential. With your experience growing, you will start to develop your own style and your interpretations will become longer and stronger.

Intensity.

It is very important to remember that the art of interpreting a reading depends on many subtleties, and the intensity of the cards drawn must be changed in function of the importance of the question, and also because of the influence of the cards surrounding each one.

The first point seems obvious. Doing daily readings is nice to learn the cards, but we don't see many major events happening on a day to day basis. After all we don't get a new job everyday, and neither do to get into a new relationship to leave one.

These kinds of reading, or mundane questions require

you to tone down the meanings. Success for your day might mean small pleasant things happening, and Ruin will not mean that you ruined your life, you might just have dealt with a few actions gradually diminishing your happiness for the day. Always adapt the intensity of your cards to the situation you face and your question.

Another important aspect is the cards interacting with each other. For instance, a very bad situation giving the card Success as a result might not mean the biggest success possible, but rather a successful situation, but by not much. Same as something brilliant terminating, for example, with Ruin, will show a small degradation, while a bad situation followed by Ruin might show a total annihilation of your situation. There is always a balance to find, and that one is mostly given by your intuition.

Don't skip cards.

When learning a new oracle, it is normal to not know everything there is to know about it. Often, difficulties start when dealing with what is commonly called "bad cards" or "negative cards", all these cards leading to an unfavorable situation or outcome. Especially when they are found in favorable positions in a spread. Or the reverse, cards deemed "positive" in an unfavorable position.

What happens often when starting, is the tendency to skip over these or minimize them because of a lack of comprehension. That's quite normal, as knowing all the subtleties of what the cards mean comes with time and experience.

If I had only one piece of advice to give, it is to read all the cards. Never skip a card. Take extra time to try to understand what is happening.

Maybe there is a problem with being overwhelmed when

seeing all the cards of a spread on the table. There is a solution for this: put all the cards face down, and turn them one at the time, interpreting as much as you can about that card before going to the next. Try to spend the same amount of time with each card. Acting this way will certainly make you a better reader.

Look for precision.

After learning for a while, it generally becomes difficult for most of us to find questions to practice with. When this happens, we tend to ask vague questions which often turn into what we could call a daily reading: what will happen today in my life. Or something similar.

Doing general daily readings when learning can be nice, but at the same time they can quickly become problematic for your progress in a few different ways. First, after doing them for a while, we start getting used to see some cards appearing always in the same kind of situations, and it becomes difficult to see them in a different context.

For instance, we might associate Amor with the love department, and every time we see that card, we will associate it with a sentimental situation. This is where doing readings without a precise question can hurt your growth. We start losing perspective in how we interpret the cards, locking them in a particular interpretation.

Another problem is that not many life-changing events happen in our lives everyday. Most of what is happening during the day is mundane. And this where the difficulty lies when doing readings with a too general question, we have difficulties determining what is going on, and as a result our responses become vague.

If would be much better, in order to give a meaningful and precise interpretation, to ask more precise questions.

Vague questions will always give vague answers. Instead of asking "what should I know for today", it would be better to ask for instance "how will be my meeting today", or "how will be my evening with my friend", etc. Giving a context will allow you to be more precise, and you will also learn to be more flexible because you will have to interpret your cards in different situations.

Journal your readings.

Journaling is very important for two different reasons.

First, divination is extremely personal, as we all have our own personality and a different life experience. As such, a book serves as a reference when you begin your journey with a pack of cards, but with time, we all get our own take on what such or such card means, and these definitions will evolve with us all our life. It is important for you to write down your own feelings and how you see the different cards, even if these impressions differ greatly from what you find in books. With time, your journal will become your own book with your own take on the cards.

Second, your journal will allow you to keep a record of the readings you did. By documenting them you are able to revisit them later and verify what happened compared to what was your interpretation. This is an important step when learning, as this will allow you to understand where you went wrong in some readings and most importantly why. Sometimes also, events happen progressively after having done a reading, and journaling will allow you to update the situation regularly and follow closely what is happening.

Over time, your journal will become an invaluable source of knowledge. If you want to become accurate in your readings, the only way that I know of, is to keep a record of your readings and observations, as the feedback you get will allow you to correct what is causing you trouble.

Practice makes perfect.

As a final advice for this chapter, practice, practice again, and practice more...

While a theoretical knowledge of the oracle is awesome, it will never replace the practical experience you can gain with your cards. The more you read, and I mean the cards, not books, the more your intuition will take over and the more your rapport with these cards will develop.

A Humanistic Cartomancy

When we look at cartomancy, we quickly realize that the term includes a wide range of different views, which can go from divination to the psychological study of the person, with all the intermediate possibilities, in which we can find clairvoyance, guiding the consultant in his choices, or personal development.

This book, as well as the tone I give to the definitions of the cards and to the spreads, is, of course, influenced by the way I see life in general: I am not a fatalist.

Unlike those who think that our lives are predestined and that everything is written when we are born, I am convinced that much of what happens to us is a consequence of our actions. Our past actions influence our present, and how we act in the present will have a significant impact on our future. Unlike a predestined future, this is called free will.

This is why I advocate the use of humanistic cartomancy, focused on the person coming for a consultation.

It is of course obvious that any consultation will talk about the future and in what direction the consultant's problems will be headed. But what would be the point of predicting what will happen if we do not look in detail at the consequences of this presupposed future on the life of our consultant, or if we do not analyze the different possibilities he or she is facing, in order to give him or her the best chances of getting what he or she wants?

Instead of focusing solely on predictions, my consultations are therefore focused first on the person who comes to seek help. This way of working allows the consultant to be refocused in a context of responsibility and freedom, presenting him or her with possible options rather than assertions.

This is what we call free will, the consultant remains master of his or her choices, and can decide to act or not based on the information given.

Take for example the classic question that every practitioner regularly gets in their practice: Will he come back? What's the point of answering yes or no? To say that the other is not coming back would be a risk to get the consultant more depressed without foundation or proposing a solution. And saying that the other will come back could give false hopes, as coming back often brings the same problems that existed before the separation.

All our consultant wants is for the partner to come back, telling themselves that everything will be fine this time. But we all know that's not necessarily the case. First understanding why the situation has deteriorated to the point that the other person is leaving, and then seeing how it might possibly be possible to remedy it seems much more useful to me. This would provide a solid basis for a discussion on how to address the problem.

After, we can try to determine the consequences for the consultant if the partner returns, as well as if he does not return. All of these elements will allow our querent to make informed decisions.

Part 2
A Closer Look at the Cards

Because we need a common language

The Composition of the Oracle

The oracle Belline was originally designed by the Mage Edmond in the 19th century. It was discovered by accident and made public much later, in the 1960s, by Marcel Belline. You can read more about the life of Marcel Belline and how his discovered these cards in Annex 2, page 246.

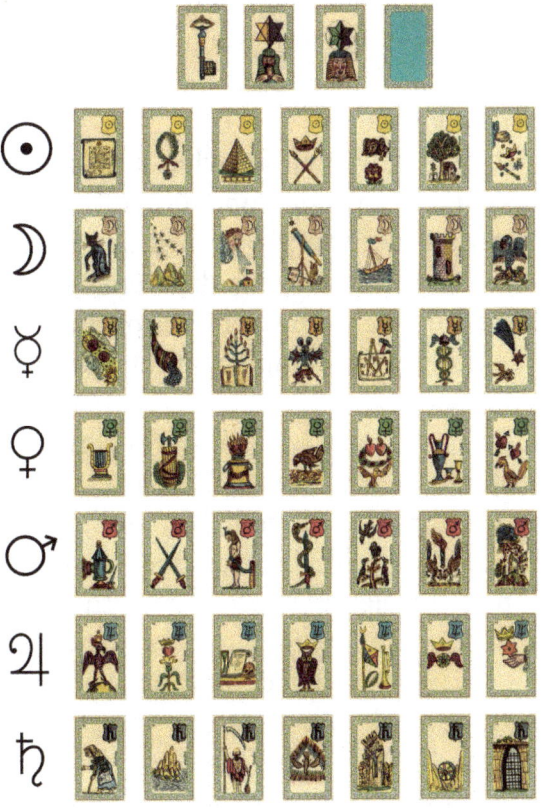

The oracle is composed of the fifty-two original cards as drawn by Mage Edmond, with forty-nine of them associated with a planet, and an optional additional card, the Blue card, added later by Marcel Belline. We will go over the reasons to use the blue card or not when giving its detailed description.

The first four cards of the oracle are not associated with a planet. Destiny, Man's Star, Woman's Star, and the Blue card, can be seen as outliers and having a very important role.

The other forty-nine cards are divided into seven series of seven cards, with each different series associated to a particular planet. We find the seven planets that were usually known at the time this oracle was designed and used in astrology, the Sun, the Moon, Mercury, Venus, Mars, Jupiter, and Saturn. Each card has also a simple image, a number, and a keyword.

For each planet, we will see what it means in mythology, definitions used in astrology, and its symbology. From these, the characteristics of the planet will be given, followed by how we can use these with the different cards. Please note that the astronomical characteristics of the planets will not be given, as they have no impact on the interpretation of the cards.

For each card, there will be first a formal definition of what the name means, taken from the Merriam-Webster and the Cambridge dictionaries, followed by a few keywords. These will be followed with a symbolic description of the elements present on the image. All these taken together will allow for a general definition of the card and how it could be used in divination.

Last, there will be sections showing how these definitions can be used as an asset, as a problem, as advice, as an evolution, and as an outcome.

As a last remark, the official version of the oracle Belline is published only in the French language. I use a straight translation of the card names to English as I am strongly convinced that the original names are a very important factor in the meaning of the cards.

1 - Destiny

(La Destinée)

*"The things that will happen in the future.
The force that some people think controls what happens in the future, and is outside of human control.
The particular state of a person thing in the future, considered as resulting from earlier events."*

Keywords: knowledge, discovery, decision to make, access, chance, success.

 On the card, we find a blue and golden key. This is a strange way to represent destiny, as a key gives us a notion of free will, totally opposite of fate, usually attributed to destiny. Keys allow us to open and close doors, and thus allow us access to places that were restricted, or inversely allow us to close doors, protecting places and objects. Having the key, as as result, gives us a feeling of freedom of choice: use it or not. Maybe the destiny of which Mage Edmond is referring to is something that can be obtained through our actions and decisions.

Something that seems very important in the key drawn on this card, is the pin, that is inserted into the lock: it shows a book. In that aspect, the key represented is not only opening real doors, but also doors giving us access to knowledge we did not have previously.

We all have different notions of faith and what is predetermined or not in our lives, and whatever our feelings could be, the key always represents something important, a "key" event happening to us or around us.

As a result, we can see "destiny" as something important happening in our lives. Either it is predestined or not, the key gives us the capability to open doors, material or not, and as such give us a sense of control in our lives.

As an asset

Having the key gives you power to act, as it allows you open doors and acquire the necessary knowledge for what you are seeking. Whatever is your goal, Destiny gives you a big advantage over others.

As a problem

To give you an image, it is very difficult to to move forward when there is a closed door in front of you and you don't have the key to open it: you are lacking means or knowledge to be able to reach a successful outcome.

Another possibility is that someone else has that key symbolically, giving that person more control over your situation than you; or different goals, putting them in a much better position to achieve success.

As advice

Destiny invites you to action, to use your good judgment. You have the key, you can use it to symbolically unlock the doors needed to move your plans forward. This can take different forms, such as doing certain specific actions or seeking a particular knowledge.

As evolution
Important events will certainly happen, ones over which you have some level of control. Opportunities are seized, your free will and freedom of action allow you to make your goals progress.

As outcome
New doors are opening to you, and these new possibilities can be considered as a success. The key is in your hand, you control your destiny and what your projects become.

2 - The Man's Star
3 - The Woman's Star

Étoile de l'Homme

-

Étoile de la Femme

As an exception, these two cards will be analyzed together, as they have many similarities.

Keywords for the Man's Star: masculinity, virility, force, action, energy.

Keywords for the Woman's Star: femininity, patience, comprehension, empathy.

The cards picture respectively a portrait of a man and a woman, with a star on top.

We will see in several cards, such as for instance Inconstancy (13), that Mage Edmond could draw faces  correctly. There has to be a reason why he did not in these cards, the faces looks like a mask.

Something that was very popular at the time the oracle Belline was created, was a theater show made with puppets and called Guignol. The faces on the two cards remind us of these puppets. Although often thought of as children's entertainment, Guignol had a sharp wit and some linguistic verve, making it very satirist of themes current for that time, and drawing on the concerns of the working class.

The hairstyle looks Egyptian, which is not surprising as all things relating to Egyptology were quite popular in the middle of the 19th century.

The star on top of the man's head represents the Star of David, a symbol first of Jewish identity and Judaism. The symbol might also have cabalistic roots, and has been associated with Jewish mysticism and magic. But if we go back to mid 19th century, the Star of David was not only associated with Judaism, it was also possible to find it as a symbol in many religious communities, for example Buddhism, and Hinduism.

The star on the woman's head represents the Seal of Solomon. The Seal of Solomon, or Signet of Solomon, is a ring that was attributed to King Solomon. It was used among other things to control evil spirits.

On a practical level, the Man's Star can represent the querent if he is a man, or any man involved in the situation you are inquiring about.

The Woman's Star can represent the querent if she is a woman, or any woman involved in the situation you are inquiring about.

For gay couples, as there are only two people cards in the oracle, each one of these will be assigned to one partner.

In particular cases these cards can also go beyond representing people, and be seen as traits of character.

As an asset

You or someone important you know are key to what is going on and the capability of acting in a positive way.

As a problem

You or someone important to your situation are hurting any kind of progress.

As advice

Use the qualities described by the card. For the Man's Star, use your force, be active, spend energy to allow your projects to move forward. For the Woman's Star, be patient, try to comprehend what is going on.

As evolution

You, or someone close to you and involved in the context in which you find yourself, will prove important to the development of your projects.

As outcome

The outcome of the situation you find yourself in will have a major impact on you or someone else involved.

The Blue Card

(La Carte Bleue)

The Blue card is the most controversial one in the deck, as it is completely different from the other ones. It does not have a number, a name, or even an image. We only find a blue uniform background.

There is no agreement among practitioners on the inclusion of the blue card or not. On that subject, even Belline gives a very vague indication in the little white book accompanying the deck. He writes verbatim "An additional plain blue card is specially beneficent and can be used as a substitution card."

So, either it is beneficent, or used as substitution if you lose one card.

I tried both options when I started using the oracle, and my personal conclusion was to not use it. I don't like that notion that one out of the fifty-three cards is like a "free get out of jail" type of card, telling you all is wonderful when there is no equivalent in the opposite direction. For me, that would make the oracle unbalanced and leaning toward a positive side. I also prefer to use more nuanced cards, like the other fifty-two, as I rarely see a problem as going 100% in one direction. I find it also too different form the other cards, and it does not seem to belong to the deck.

In addition, the card was not part of the original deck, it was added by Belline a century later. If the Mage Edmond, creator of the oracle, did not design it, I don't see why I would use the oracle differently.

Anyway, like most other things, I would advise you to try both cases, using it and not, and decide what you prefer. If you decide to use it, the interpretation is quite simple, as follows.

As an asset

You have all you the qualities and tools needed to succeed in your endeavors.

As a problem

This is the position in a reading where the blue card becomes problematic. As it shows so much positivity and potential, when it becomes a problem, we need to reverse these qualities, and the card will show that major difficulties are present, your chances of being successful are close to none as powerful forces are acting against you.

As advice

Be positive, do not be afraid to commit to your objectives and take the necessary steps to move forward, as chance is on your side.

As evolution

Your projects are evolving beautifully. No major setback happens, everything evolves smoothly.

As outcome
You can expect a complete and successful realization of your projects.

The Sun

The Sun is the star at the center of our Solar system, estimated to be 4.6 billion years old. It is the center around which all the planets revolve. They are, in order from the closest to the farther away, Mercury, Venus, Earth, Mars, Jupiter, Saturn, Uranus, and Neptune.

In many religions and spiritual systems, the Sun has always played a major role, providing deities that were central to many belief systems all round the world. The Sun was very quickly associated with the concept of a God creator of all things. It was central to many old civilizations, including the Egyptians, the Incas and the Aztecs.

Among these many solar cults, the Sun has played an active role and is linked to the masculine archetype, being associated to a strong and dependable energy.

In astrology, the Sun represents the self, our drive, ego, and pride, it is our basic identity. The sun sign describes our overall attitude and spirit. It is the most important planet in our chart to assess our personality, as it symbolizes one's will and sense of vitality.

Symbolically, the Sun has always played a central role in all philosophical traditions, all the symbolic and spiritual legends that men have conceived and disseminated. After all, this seems normal for a star that provides us every day with warmth and light, two elements necessary to produce life and sustain us.

It is no wonder, in that case, that all the cards placed under the sign of the Sun inspire decorum. They perfectly carry the attributes embodied by the Sun: warmth, light, energy, good news and success.

If we look at the seven cards the Sun rules, they will be under the influence of its warmth and energy, a favorable influence. We can find its qualities represented as fertility in Nativity (4), accomplishments in Success (5), personal development and fulfillment in Elevation (6), glory, bravery and recognition in Honors (7), altruism in Thought-Friendship (8), good health and recharging oneself in Countryside-Health (9), joy and happiness in Gifts (10).

4 - Nativity

(La Nativité)

*"The process or circumstances of being born.
A horoscope at or of the time of one's birth.
The place of origin"*

Keywords: beginning, birth, something starting, new project, emergence.

 Nativity shows a yellow parchment on which we find a square horoscope with the twelve signs of the zodiac, which is a direct reference to astrology as it is very present in this oracle. The square pattern for a horoscope is an ancient representation that was abandoned later in favor of a circular design. This is one of the few cards signed by the Mage Edmond, the creator of the oracle.
 In this particular instance, the astral theme is almost empty, the only planets we can find are the Sun and the Moon. An empty horoscope can certainly be an analogy for a situation where "nothing is written yet", something that is just starting, when no important event has happened yet.

We can see Nativity as being often the beginning of something new. The card can represent a person in a state of mind of openness, welcoming what is new around them, and ready to embrace with faith life and what it brings them.

As such, Nativity will represent new projects, new events, something that is planned but for which no realization took place yet.

As an asset

This is a favorable time for you to start something new, whether it's fresh ideas, new projects, or emerging situations. Now is the time for you to start working on creating what you imagine you are capable of achieving.

As a problem

As Nativity is a card showing new beginnings, something starting in general, it expresses difficulties to start a new project, or eventually how to come up with new ideas. You are trying to start something, but it is lacking so much planning or organization that you find yourself into the impossibility to move forward with your ideas.

As advice

Nativity begs you to bring something new into any situation you are involved with. It could be in the form of new ideas or new actions, anything bringing something fresh to your situation. As it evokes everything related to new beginnings, you should therefore make decisions allowing you to continue your situation on new bases. Take the opportunity to reconsider certain things in order to benefit from the dynamic carried by this card.

As the planet influencing Nativity is the Sun, this might also be the right time to put some energy and resources into something new, unrelated to your current situation.

As evolution

The direction taken by your situation seems favorable to bring forward new possibilities, important perspectives that you might consider but which have not yet materialized. Nativity shows the potential for those to assert themselves and come into shape in a more concrete way.

As outcome

Nativity can show success to the extent that it forecasts the birth of something important: it might be material, spiritual, or anything else that you value. As a Sun card, without predicting what will happen next, it forecasts that the steps you are taking will lead to a successful outcome.

What is important with Nativity is to have confidence in the future as it often refers to early success in your efforts, bringing you to a point where you can envisage moving forward with the next step.

5 - Success

(Réussite)

*"Favorable or desired outcome.
The attainment of wealth, favor, or eminence."*

Keywords: success, rewards, favorable outcome, victory, profit, retribution.

    The card is represented by a laurel wreath, from which hangs a ribbon and a medal. These are a direct references to the rewards and honors this card brings.
    The laurel wreath is a symbol of victory, honor, and peace. It was a symbol of the Greek god Apollo and the leaf itself was believed to have spiritual and physical cleansing abilities. Ancient Greeks awarded laurel wreaths to victors in the olympics and poetic competitions. Roman emperors and military commanders often wore them after a battle. Still to this day, the laurel wreath is often given by universities at master ceremonies, or found on diplomas, as a sign of success and mastery.
    A ribbon and a medal are issued to commemorate a

person, action, or event, and given as a reward to an act of bravery, merit, or similar action. The shape of the medal reminds us of the "iron cross", a medal that was typically awarded for outstanding bravery.

As we can deduct from the symbolism of these objects, Success will show a perseverant person, who will not stop when faced with obstacles. It shows someone who is rewarded because they could reach their objectives, or someone who stands out for their abilities to move forward and use their potential in the best possible way. It will show a person who is charismatic, warm, having the potential to succeed, all qualities that the Sun brings also as a planet.

As an asset

It shows a lot of potential, that you have the capabilities needed to succeed in any situation where you are involved. This is certainly one of the best cards to have as an asset, as it shows that everything works in your favor, you have all the tools and the courage needed to succeed and reach your goals.

As a problem

The card shows that you are not, for the moment, in a position to attain any form of success. This might be due to lack of courage or perseverance, or some external elements playing against you, but you are facing many difficulties to move forward.

As advice

In order to be successful, you have to act as someone successful, you must assert your own potential or your ideas with the swagger found in all triumphant people. Be bold, Success invites you to take action with the attitude of someone who is confident.

As evolution

Success is of course a very good omen when looking at the evolution of a situation, as what is dealt with evolves in a bright and promising direction. Of course, it is still up to you to provide enough energy to continue working on your projects, but the card shows that they are taking a favorable turn.

As outcome

Success indicates that your efforts will pay off and that you will reach your goal. With the energy and light of the Sun, everything is possible in order to bring a satisfying outcome to your situation. Problems are solved, projects will succeed.

6 - Elevation

(Elévation)

*"The height to which something is elevated.
The angular distance of something above the horizon.
The height above the level of the ground."*

Keywords: ascension, gain of altitude, global view, progression, ambition.

The card shows a pyramid, and a ladder laying on the ground.

The pyramid has an interesting shape, symbolically it can represent the Earth's foundation, square at the bottom, while the pointed top represents the path to higher realms of consciousness. The triangular sides were also believed to represent the rays of the Sun and its pointed top was seen as a representation of the sky or the heavens.

The ladder laying on the ground shows that the querent has the tools at their disposition to elevate themselves and reach a higher position. But as most things in life, a effort will be required to reach their goals, and it will probably happen step by step.

The symbolism of these elements shows the greatness of this card, where the main concept is the one of improvement or elevating oneself. This development can of course be on a spiritual, social, personal, or material level.

Another aspect to note with this card, is that by elevating ourselves in a particular situation, we are able to see what is happening from a distance, and with a higher perspective.

As an asset

Your experience and judgment allow you to gain perspective on the situation you are involved with. As a result, you are able to take some distance from the the day to day details and see what is happening more globally. That higher perspective allows you to look at your circumstances with objectivity.

As a problem

Elevation will show difficulties to progress, to attain your objectives. This is probably due to the fact that you stay too close to your problems, your point of view becomes too narrow, and it becomes difficult to see your situation globally, you lack objectivity.

You might also be dealing with so many down to earth problems that your projects cannot grow anymore.

As advice

Elevation shows a lack of progress in achieving your goals. This is probably because you stay too close to your problems, your point of view becomes too narrow and it becomes difficult for you to a global view of what is going on, you lack objectivity. As a result, you cannot easily take the next step necessary to develop your situation.

As evolution

Your projects are progressing and reaching a higher level, moving closer to realization. This is probably due to the fact that you have a better view of what is going on. Indeed, by seeing your context more globally, you're able to better understand your circumstances and gain a better perspective from which you can react more effectively.

As outcome

Elevation expresses more a notion of reaching another level or getting a few steps closer to your goals, rather than a complete success. With this card, we are looking more about improvement rather than a complete resolution.

Think, for instance, about your relationship getting to another level, or getting a promotion at work. These do not show a complete satisfactory outcome, you are dealing more with a substantial progress.

7 - Honors

(Honneurs)

*"Good name or public esteem.
A showing of usually merited respect.
Privilege."*

Keywords: recognition, acceptance, distinction, gratitude, pride, notoriety.

We find a crown with two scepters crossing each other below it, two symbols of authority and power.

The crown on top of the card evokes a sense of royalty, of someone having universal power. In the context of this card, we can see the crown as representing an honorific title, as it was usually reserved for royalty.

Below it, we find two scepters, one has a spherical pommel and on the other a hand with the index finger outstretched. Together, they represent a symbol of universal power and authority. Similar to the the crown, a scepter was first and foremost given to rulers and used in ceremonial occasions.

There is a discernible difference between card (5) Success and Honors. While Success showed a favorable outcome to a situation, Honors deals more in the circumstances around which that success is obtained. It shows a form of personal elevation which is only accessible for the ones who act with morals and principles, and there is a notion of respect given to the person.

Honors can also represent a talented person, one who is acclaimed for what they can do. As such, it represents someone who distinguished themselves in the past.

As an asset

You are in a flourishing period, and nothing seems able to stop you. That allows you to be recognized for the efforts you put forward in solving your problems, or the situations you are involved with. Honors certainly shows a very dynamic person, acting in a righteous way and with great power of conviction, courage, and honesty.

As a problem

The solutions you're looking for might be difficult to obtain in an honorable way. As a result, pride, self-esteem, overconfidence, and recklessness have a tendency of being put forward to try to resolve conflicts. There is a tendency of using morally corrupt means to try to achieve some objectives, and acting more as a despot than a just leader.

As advice

Honors advises you to put forward your ability to take command of the situation you find yourself in, and show your leadership in how you act. After all, the card is before anything else about recognition and morality in the way you act to solve your issues. In that regard, try not to act too quickly or with a lack of accountability. You should always emphasize the righteousness of your character.

As evolution

Confidence in the situation you are involved in will grow, as you are well-judged and appreciated by others. As some form of recognition is coming, it will allow you to act decisively and show you qualities of leadership and righteousness in your actions. As a result, your projects are moving forward in a pleasant way, recognition for your efforts is coming.

As outcome

Being recognized and honored by your peers is certainly a good sign for the progress of your projects, which are at least moving in the right direction. As you are celebrated for your efforts, you can be confident that the situation you are dealing with will be resolved in your favor. Not only is there a notion of a positive outcome with Honors, but also one that can you can be proud of.

8 - Thought-Friendship

(Pensée - Amitié)

"An individual act or product of thinking; something in the mind; a reasoning power.
The state of being friends; a relationship between friends.
A state of enduring affection, esteem, and trust between two people."

Keywords: altruism, fidelity, protection, benevolence, loyalty, sincerity, harmony.

The keyword "friendship" reminds us of feelings of affection and sympathy that develop between two people. That's certainly the reason why we can see the head of a dog in the middle of the card. Already at the time of Greeks and Romans, dogs were valued for their faithfulness and bravery. They symbolized loyalty and for that reason, dogs have always been accepted as domestic animals. After all, there is a reason why we often hear that the dog is man's best friend, a loyal companion.

In that context, the other keyword, "thought", should be

understood, not especially in the rationalization and understanding of ideas, but rather in a more affective context, the one where we're thinking about someone else, with an affective connotation. On a more symbolic aspect, the flower drawn on the card is a pansy, a flower evoking beautiful thoughts, as they are often associated with memories, love, affection, especially in the sentimental domain.

These two symbols express nicely the main concepts behind this card, the ones of friendship and loyalty to other people, and the innocence and naturalness in relations.

As an asset

One of your main qualities is that you are very welcoming with people, and you can start new friendships, people tend to appreciate you. That allows you to easily establish new contacts, that can help you in realizing your projects. In these new contacts, loyalty becomes important, as either you find people ready to help you or having the kind of expertise you are lacking.

As a problem

You find yourself isolated facing your problems. There can be two reasons for this: either you have difficulties establishing a good contact with others, or you find yourself in an unfriendly environment. Either way, this lack of support harms your plans and puts you at risk of not achieving your goals.

As advice

Thought-Friendship invites you to reach out to others and behave in an altruistic way. Your goals would benefit from at least having the support of people who can help you, either directly by their expertise, or by bringing their moral support. In order to accomplish this, you must of course show qualities such as empathy and loyalty toward others. Be open to others, your social network can help you.

As evolution

One of the best consequences of Thought-Friendship is the avoidance of tensions and conflicts with others. That allows you to progress towards your goals in a peaceful atmosphere. Effectively, you find yourself in a climate where trust and loyalty reign.

As outcome

A pleasant atmosphere allows your projects to reach some form of success, as it indicates feelings of confidence and safety in the way they are dealt with. The way you allow yourself to easily establish communications with others allows you to gain some stability and a sense of accomplishment. Your life is brightened by the bond of friendship you share with others.

9 - Countryside-Health

(Campagne - Santé)

*"A rural area; the land and scenery of a rural area.
The general condition of the body; a condition in which someone or something is thriving or doing well."*

Keywords: vacation, leisure, relaxation, nature, tranquility, rejuvenation, serenity.

On the card we find a house, a tree and a flower, which seems to be a lily. The dwelling is a place where we feel secure and "at home", protected by the walls that surround us. The building protects its inhabitants from external forces and gives them shelter when outside conditions are not favorable.

The tree has always been a symbol of health and vitality, something growing slowly, but strong and deep-rooted. The lily has also been a symbol of purity, a flower that takes time to cultivate. It also represents an emblem of royalty; think for instance of "fleur de lys" among the French royal family before the revolution of 1789.

Countryside-Health inspires calm, serenity, and rest. Countryside must be understood in opposition to city life, where activity and noise are constant. Here we find a quiet atmosphere where body and spirit can rest and heal, far away from any source of stress. The card is intended to be reassuring for the consultant by placing him or her in a safe and secure position.

As such, it can represent a person feeling great and rested, physically and morally. At a minimum, it will show a quiet lifestyle, lived in a serene atmosphere.

As an asset

You find yourself in a quiet environment, where there is no conflict. That allows you to face your problems and difficulties with a serene mind, one which is devoid of external noise and influences. Confidence reigns, you can stay quiet and optimistic, without wasting your energy in quarrels.

As a problem

In regards to your question, you take too much time to relax and you look at your problems with too much detachment. That kind of inactivity becomes problematic as you are probably facing a situation that requires some action from your part. You are overconfident and optimistic, to the point where you take too much distance from what is happening around you.

As advice

You are in a position where you should take the time to relax and cool down before taking any action. Be patient, act slowly, wait until you feel secure in your position before doing anything. Sometimes, not acting and letting things go without your involvement will provide the best result.

As evolution

Countryside-Health shows that your projects are evolving smoothly but slowly, you might even feel that they take too long to come to realization. Effectively, not much action is happening, the mood is more into healing or repairing what needs to be fixed, rather than radical action. Calm and tranquility will be conductive to the well-being of your projects.

As outcome

Sun as planet already indicates a successful direction for your projects, as it will provide enough energy for their realization. But with this card, you should not expect a situation where much is happening. You will find yourself in a quiet, serene situation, one where no major or important changes happen. The time is more into fixing or healing the existing problems.

A final word of warning: even if there is progress, you might not appreciate the outcome in some situations. If you are looking for a resounding progress, like for instance when doing a job interview, you might find yourself in a situation where you performed well, but maybe too detached to get what you were looking for.

10 - Gifts

(Présents)

*"A notable capacity, talent, or endowment.
Something voluntary transferred by one person to another without compensation; the act, right, or power of giving."*

Keywords: gratification, generosity, retribution, gain, favors, donation.

One hand coming out of a cloud is giving away seven coins, a crown, a medal, and a scepter.

First, we can see the hand as a "heavenly hand" extending from the cloud, and opening to give us all these items falling from it. A "heavenly" intervention would be an act we do not expect and providing us with something tangible.

If we look at what is given, coins represent material wealth. We can expect, when receiving them, to have an easier life as they provide us with the possibility to fulfill our basic material needs.

The crown, the scepter, and the medal are three

important honorific distinctions. A medal is given to recognize our bravery and is typically awarded as recognition of our actions. The scepter and the crown remind us of card (7) Honors, where we found also these same objects, symbolically representing a personal elevation given to us, as a reward for our morals and how we did act.

Gifts represents all the presents and good things we are given in life. It can also be how we are recognized morally, or something more mundane, something providing us with some material wealth.

By extension, Gifts can also represent a person who cares about our well-being, and is ready to provide us with what we need.

As an asset

The situation you find yourself in is such that everything you need to reach your goals is symbolically given to you. There is not much effort you need to do, as you can count on the generosity of others to help you in your quest, allowing you to have a lot of means to solve your current issues.

As a problem

As Gifts represents first all the favors and material assets you would need to solve your problems, finding this card in an unfavorable position becomes problematic. It shows the lack of resources at your disposal, suppressing the help and support you could get from others. As a result, you are left alone, without much at your disposal, to try to fix your problems.

As advice

You should be generous and considerate, as the card emphasizes the importance of rewards, which can be moral or material. Generosity means that you should be able to give without expecting anything back.

We could also consider the reverse aspect, where you are the one receiving. In that case, do not hesitate to ask for the help you need, which can be moral, material, or by the intervention of other people, as the card forewarns that what you are asking for is available somewhere.

As evolution

The situation evolves favorably for you, people are ready to help you, and it is up to you to see and recognize the chances and opportunities coming your way. These opportunities can be in the form of people helping you, capable of influencing the situation in your favor, or some material or financial help.

As outcome

Gifts predicts success, as the card concept is one of enrichment, of things given to you. In this regard, there are opportunities to be seized, and you get rewarded by receiving some form of power or authority, or some financial or material advantage .

The Moon

The Moon is the only natural satellite orbiting the Earth, at a distance of approximately 239 thousand miles. The Moon is particular in the way that the same side always faces the Earth, due to the fact that it rotates exactly once per orbit, with a lunar day of 29.5 Earth days long. The Moon has a very big influence on the Earth, as its gravitational pull is the main driver of the tides.

In the oracle Belline, the Moon is considered as a planet, same as in astrology and esoteric circles.

The Moon is omnipresent in all mythologies and popular beliefs, and it is often associated with the feminine divinity. In ancient China it came under the yin principle, and in Greek mythology, it was known as the goddess Selene. The feminine influence of the Moon is certainly due to the lunar month, which corresponds to the female menstrual period.

In astrology, the Moon is the ruler of your emotions. It describes your emotional life, desires, feelings, the workings of your inner world. If the Sun gives us our spirit, the Moon gives us our soul. It rules all the subconscious events happening below the surface in our lives. Fertility, pregnancy and childbirth are also ruled by the Moon, as well as the maternal side.

Symbolically, and in opposition to the Sun, the Moon is passive as it gravitates around the Earth. It represents the feminine principle, complimentary to the masculine principle of the Sun. It is also associated with the night, its magic and mysteries, as opposed to the light of the day revealing a more objective reality. As such, it can be the world of darkness, the unknown, the unconscious.

In the same vein, the moon evokes the intimacy of the psyche and the condition of the human soul, caught between its dark side (instincts, uncontrolled passions) and its bright side (reflection, logic).

The moon also evokes change and impermanence: it is an evolving star, sometimes illuminating the night as in almost broad daylight (full moon), or fading completely to give way to darkness.

We can find these aspects represented as unreliability and darkness in Betrayal (11), unknowns in Departure (12), unseen changes and moodiness in Inconstancy (13), mystery in Discovery (14), emotions and the psyche in Water (15), family in Penates (16), and sickness in Disease (17).

11 - Betrayal

(Trahison)

*"The violation of a person's trust or confidence, of a moral standard, etc.
Revelation of something hidden or secret."*

Keywords: deception, betrayal, lack of loyalty, infidelity, lust, lack of confidence.

A cat is looking at the consultant with a mischievous look, showing its teeth and claws, tail up, ready to scratch at any unexpected moment. All signs pointing to a quick action leading to duplicity or hurt.

Sometimes associated with the devil and witches, a black cat can be frightening and quickly became in many traditions an evil being. It is often linked with a negative image and a sneaky attitude, probably due to the independence of the animal. There is also the fact that their eyes, as opposed to human eyes, allow them to see very clearly during the night. This gives to the cat a sense of assurance in the dark, of course, with it, comes imagined powers like lust, cruelty, etc.

Even today, for the most superstitious among us, crossing paths with a black cat can be a bad omen.

As an asset

You are able to detect quickly what seems wrong around you. For example, if someone tries to deceive you, or you find yourself in a situation such that you feel taken advantage of, you are capable of detecting what is going on and react.

Betrayal could also indicate that you need to think about yourself first. In that case, it might be that you need to reveal hidden information or instigate some action that will give you an advantage, even if it can hurt someone else.

As a problem

Sometimes we are our own enemy when dealing with others, Betrayal can mean that you literally betray yourself with your actions, for instance revealing information that will hurt you later, or acting in such a way that others will lose trust in you.

But often, the problem is that people are taking too much advantage of you. In order to reach their goals, they are not afraid to mislead you, or even stab you in the back. For instance, you might find people gossiping behind your back, spreading false information about you. Whatever it is, some elements or aspects of what is happening are not as they appear, and promises are not kept.

As advice

You should be careful and suspicious about what is going on around you, as Betrayal represents an unseen danger lurking. Stay away form untrustworthy people, and the ones who could abuse you using their influence.

You might also be the one using the attributes of the card. In that sense, you should probably be careful to not reveal too much about your situation. You might even suggest things that are not 100% accurate if they can give you some advantage. Sometimes, when facing some difficult situations, hiding you true intentions might be the best way to proceed forward.

As evolution

The evolution of the situation you're involved in will probably be a little bit disappointing, you should not expect that events will evolve the way you are hoping for. Betrayal really predicts a gap between what you expect and the reality of what is happening, to the point where you should reconsider your expectations.

As outcome

Betrayal will certainly leave you with a bitter taste, as you can expect some form of disappointment in what happened. There might be some misunderstanding about the situation you find yourself in, which is probably caused by the untrustworthy attitude of people surrounding you.

As expressed earlier, betrayal can also happen due to actions we did to ourselves. We might have misunderstood the situation we find ourselves in, or be too confident, and as a result act in ways that hurts us later. In that case, the outcome we expected does not happen, leaving us with a sense of disillusion caused by a lack of foresight.

12 - Departure

(Départ)

*"The action of leaving.
A deviation from a accepted, prescribed, or traditional course of action or thought.
Beginning of a planned achievement, an action, or an activity."*

Keywords: leaving behind, new projects, emancipation, freedom, renewal.

A flock of ten birds takes flight and leaves behind a mountain.

Birds have always symbolized concepts such as new beginnings, hope, and freedom. So, it seems evident to associate these ten birds leaving the mountain as a departure, an emancipation in the sense of leaving some place in order to find a new one to colonize. At the same time, a flight is often associated with some kind of elevation, as it describes our ability to elevate or distance ourselves from a situation that does not satisfy us anymore, and to try to reach something new, oftentimes still unknown to us.

If we look carefully at the mountains depicted on the card, they look very similar to the mountains found in card (47) Sterility. They are barren, there is no vegetation, no life. This could explain that the place these birds are leaving has nothing more to offer. They are moving on from a situation which has become unfortunate and in which nothing more can be gained.

As an asset

The flexibility with how you deal with any situation can be seen as an asset, as it allows you to navigate and move in a direction putting you in a more favorable position. You are ready to take a chance or to leave an unfortunate situation, even if you don't know yet where it will lead you; all you know is that this move will solidify your position.

As a problem

Departure of course describes problems related to the possibility of moving freely, or all kinds of movement in general. You know that the situation you are involved with becomes static, unhealthy, and there is nothing more to gain, but at the same time you do not have the strength or capability to leave it.

As advice

Departure invites you to evolve by leaving behind a situation that does not bring you anything good anymore. Even if you do not know yet your destination, you should not burden yourself with things from the past that do not bring you anything useful anymore, it is time to take the next step forward.

As evolution

The situation you find yourself in is not going to remain static. Departure forecasts drastic changes, changes that will make you leave the situation you are in, as you have nothing more to gain from it. Effectively, like these migratory birds are showing, there will be a departure from the current direction in which things are evolving in the hope of finding something better. It is time to move toward something else, some other idea or another path.

As outcome

Departure does not forecast a successful outcome. Together with the fact that the card is under the influence of the Moon, we can see that there are still some uncertainties in the way your situation will evolve. The only sure thing, is that some movement will happen, either by the querent leaving some situation that does not provide them with what they need anymore, or to simply start something new. But the result from that move is far from certain, as the querent does not yet know where these events will lead them.

13 - Inconstancy

(Inconstance)

"Changeability, not sticking to a predetermined course. The state or act of not staying the same, especially in opinions, behavior, or love."

Keywords: indecision, hesitation, unpredictable, versatile, movement, fluctuation, superficial.

    A head is emerging from a cloud, and is blowing in the direction of a construction on top of which a green and red flag is flying. Close to the building, we can also see a mountain.

    That depiction of a head or angel face was common during the Renaissance period, and that face blowing was a typical representation at that period of the wind. As an expression of the wind, we can easily imagine that breath, which can be light or strong depending on conditions, change direction, or suddenly differ in intensity. As such, the wind becomes a symbolic representation of changes, oftentimes unpredictable, that varies constantly in intensity and direction.

At the bottom of the card, we find a mountain and a building, both sturdy enough to resit to the elements and the wind, even a strong one. That's where we can understand some duality of the card. Even in circumstances where changes are inevitable and sometimes unforeseen, we can always find a safe harbor. In that sense, changes can become a good thing as we are offered some form of protection.

However, even if we can stay safe, Inconstancy will often represent doubts and hesitations in which way to proceed.

As an asset

You are flexible and capable of correcting easily the course of the events you're dealing with. Changes can become an asset when we adapt to them, as we can benefit from our quick reactions to fluctuations.

Inconstancy can also show itself in the way we feel protected and immune to the consequences of all the changes happening around us.

As a problem

Taking decisions is problematic for you, as you are not capable of making up your mind and taking appropriate action. You are becoming a victim of your moods and versatility, up to the point where you are uncertain in the way to proceed forward, and that hinders your capabilities to execute on what is needed.

As advice

Inconstancy advises you to stay flexible, and keep an attitude of being ready to adapt to new circumstances. It might be better for you to not decide anything too soon, and instead to maintain a neutral, undetermined attitude, one where you react to the changing elements surrounding you. Being versatile is key, and sometimes the best solution is to not act at all and let the circumstances surrounding your situation decide on the course of action.

As evolution

Inconstancy shows that the evolution of your situation will become uncertain and constantly changing. Even if you can feel yourself in a safe place during these changing circumstances, you can expect reversals of situations, making any progress difficult to control.

As outcome

Indecisions and uncertainties dominate, which makes it impossible to determinate to which level your projects will be successful or not. This does not mean failure, it just means that your projects are not headed in the direction of some stable state, as you can expect more changes and updates to happen over time, often unpredictable ones.

14 - Discovery

(Découverte)

"The process of finding information, a place, or an object, especially for the first time, or the thing that is found."

Keywords: exploration, learning something new, exploration, knowledge, understanding.

    At the center of the image, we find a telescope pointed in the direction of a star, an object that evokes the exploration of something unknown, or the discovery of new things, as the primary use of a telescope is to make objects that are far away look closer and larger.

    At the bottom of the card, we find a parchment on which are drawn a star and a crossed circle, an open book, a closed book, and an owl. The books are of course associated with knowledge, and finding here one open and one closed can relate to the fact that we are in the process of learning new things, some of them not yet discovered. As for the the owl, it has always been associated with wisdom and clairvoyance, as it can see in the dark.

All these elements bring a notion of the fact that we do not know everything, and of knowledge that we discover through observation. In that sense, Discovery can also represent some new information that we had not access to in the past.

As an asset

You are curious about what is happening around you, and that attitude gives you the possibility to accrue your knowledge about the situation you find yourself in. Effectively, you are capable of finding new elements that were missing and that can help you solve the problems you are facing.

As a problem

Some aspects of your situation are not clear to you, or you are lacking some knowledge that would be needed to face your concerns. The problem you are facing, is that you have no access to new knowledge, or are not willing to take the necessary steps to inform you better. As a result, you are left vulnerable and you might not know why.

Whit Discovery it might also happen that some crucial information is hidden from you for nefarious reasons, and you are not capable of discovering the truth.

As advice

You should be curious and open minded about what is going on around you, that will allow you to gain knowledge that was not revealed until now. Looking beyond the appearances will help you to discover what is not apparent at first view. In that sense, Discovery is more about being on the alert and reacting to new facts rather than acting.

As evolution

Your project will probably require to move in a different direction than the one planned at the beginning, and maybe corrected several times, due to new information learned or revealed. These changes might result in in very small adaptations, or a total change of direction, depending on the information discovered, and as a result the new direction will show a shift in your expectations.

As outcome

As with all the cards influenced by the Moon, Discovery does not show a clear or favorable outcome, but rather that you were missing some elements. As such, Discovery will not forecast a total success, but will indicate a moving target as more information is divulged over time, and these elements will influence the final outcome.

15 - Water

(L'Eau)

"A clear liquid, without color or taste, that forms the seas, lakes, rivers, and rain and is the basis of the fluids of living organisms."

Keywords: moodiness, emotions, journey, travel, intuition, anxieties.

A boat is sailing on a rough sea, there are strong waves around it. On top of the mast, we can see a flag with the French colors, as a reminder of the origins of the oracle.

The idea of a moving boat expresses of course first a concept of travel. But with the rough sea in which it finds itself, we can expect that travel to be difficult, possibly difficulties to keep the direction, and even uncertainties about how to reach that destination. But as the boat is still moving, there is reason enough to believe that it will get where it is headed at some point in the future.

Water is an extremely important element, as without it, life on Earth would be impossible. Symbolically, water has also always been associated with our feelings and emotions, making a strong correlation between this card and its planet, the Moon. As a result, the travel represented on the card can be symbolic, showing how our emotions and moodiness can affect the way we move toward our goals.

As an asset

Your feelings work in your favor and give you an advantage in handling the situation in which you find yourself. It is important to highlight your sensitivity, your emotions and your intuition in your decisions.

Also, even if you find yourself in an unfavorable climate, where the elements are working against you, you do not hesitate to continue moving towards your goal.

As a problem

Water shows a difficulty from your part to rein-in your emotions, there is a sense of hypersensitivity hurting your chances of reaching your goals. As a result, you lack clarity, and your moods affect negatively the way you deal with others. Due to your emotivity, you can expect many detours and delays in your projects.

As advice

Water advises to be careful with the way you deal with your emotions, but it would still be preferable to act similarly to this boat, set sail to your destination, whatever happens around you. Even if the water is agitated, the boat is still moving toward the port is it trying to reach, advising you to do the same, you should start or continue your projects, whatever the odds.

As evolution

Progress is sluggish, you are moving toward your goal

slowly but surely. By the symbolic nature of water and the rough seas around the boat, you can expect delays and difficulties to maintain a firm direction. As a warning, you should allow enough time for delays and dealing with the emotional aspects of your situation.

As outcome

Water, together with the influence of the Moon, is a card symbolizing uncertainty, emotional fluctuations and anxieties, and as a result the rough sea can represent difficulties to move forward. When encountering Water, do not expect an easy resolution for your problems, but rather a work in progress, surrounded by a heavily charged emotional climate. Some efforts are still needed to reach a definitive outcome.

16 Penates

(Les Pénates)

"The Roman god of the household worshipped in close connection with Vesta and the Lares."

Keywords: home, security, building, shelter, safe place, family.

In the times of the Romans, the penates were household gods who were protecting the whole house. They referred to several deities associated with the home, and were invoked in domestic rituals, for instance during family meals. Each house had a shrine with their images. They were also worshipped privately as protectors of individual households, and publicly as protectors of the Roman Empire.

On the card, we find a tower, a construction that seems sturdy, a good protection for what is inside. As such, the card can represent a shelter, a place where we can protect ourselves and prosper in security. It also represents a place where we feel secure from external elements.

As an asset

You are acting from a secure place and a familiar environment, where you can safely work on what your situation requires in order to move forward. This work, of course, is more of a preparatory style than real action, something you do without showing it outside of your close environment. All this can help you to be in a position of force when what you are dealing with will requite some action.

As a problem

Feeling too safe and secure can sometimes become problematic, as that stability can give you a feeling that nothing can hurt you. Effectively, too much comfort and too much security are responsible for the fact that you tend to not act when facing the problems you are involved with.

Too much familiarity with your environment or the people around you do not encourage you to face risks and try new things. As a result, you remain too static and do not act quickly enough when needed.

As advice

Penates encourage you to slow down, find a peaceful place where you feel safe, and take the time to look quietly at your problems, instead of reacting in a more forceful way. Therefore, take a step back and rely on your close environment or family to help you find solutions. Nothing beats the feeling of being "at home" when facing some choices.

As evolution

A quick evolution cannot be expected with Penates, but rather something marked with a feeling of tranquility, routine, being safe and secure in how everything is moving forward. You can expect to see a slow development, with not much energy spent.

As outcome

Penates can be a good omen or not depending on what you expect. If the actions you undertake should require a quiet and stable result, you will be satisfied with the outcome. But if you expect a result that necessitates movement or a situation evolving a lot, you will feel disappointed.

Effectively, the walls offer a familiar and protective environment, but where not much activity happens. You can expect to find yourself in a period favorable to develop new ideas and new solutions, in a safe and tranquil environment. Take your time, do not enterprise anything hastily, your situation is solidifying itself in a safe environment.

The Moon

17 - Disease

(Maladie)

"A condition of the living animal, or plant body, or of one of its parts that impairs normal functioning and is typically manifested by distinguishing signs and symptoms. A harmful development."

Keywords: dysfunction, inconvenience, trouble, imbalance, displeasure.

Two animals are drawn on the card, they look like a vulture and a toad.

Toads are traditionally associated with negative symbols. They are commonly viewed as demonic creatures, often magical yet evil, and as such can represent illness or any form of disease.

Vultures, on the other hand, symbolize in many civilizations qualities such as patience, death, rebirth, and protection. These birds are mostly known for flying high in the sky, waiting for an animal to die and eating their carcass.

On the card, we see the vulture, wings deployed, landing

on the toad. When this happens, we know that the bird is going to feast on its victim. As an analogy, we can see that act similar to a positive intervention where the bird removes what is diseased or dead, allowing us to find relief.

Disease announces obstacles and difficulties, dealing with something unhealthy around us, but nothing that the querent is unable to manage.

As an asset

Disease shows the ability to detect what is wrong, dysfunctional or imbalanced in the situation you are involved with. As a result, it allows you to take action and remove or minimize the negative aspects surrounding you.

As a problem

You find yourself in a dysfunctional situation where reigns imbalance and an unhealthy climate. This environment is affecting you up to the point where it prevents you from moving forward as you would like and attaining your goal. Solving your problems becomes difficult, this situation puts a strain on your morals and your motivation diminishes due to anguish and a lack of confidence.

As advice

First, you should look for the aspects of your situation which are not functioning correctly: all these areas where you find dysfunction or something unhealthy in the sense of not being useful anymore or not working at all in your favor. Just let all these aspects come to the surface, in order to better observe what challenges you are facing, and later to bring some remedy to solve them, even if by doing so there is some discomfort.

As evolution
As Disease relates to dysfunctional areas and unhealthiness among other things, your projects are not going to easily evolve in a straightforward manner. They will be riddled with problems, difficult situations that you will have to take care of. The danger of finding yourself in an unhealthy situation becomes high and it might be burdensome to get out of it.

As outcome
The type of dysfunction Disease evokes, together with the influence of the Moon, does not bode well for a desired outcome. As the name indicates, the situation you find yourself in is "sick", and as a result there is still a lot to do before being able to find a remedy to what is happening. This might manifest itself sometimes in challenges and inconveniences that you have to deal with, but more often in something more troublesome.

Mercury

Mercury is the planet closest to the Sun, and the smallest of the solar system. Being so close, the Sun appears almost 3.5 times bigger than on the surface of the Earth.

In mythology, Mercury is the Roman version of the Greek god Hermes, who was the god creating a link between heaven and Olympus, and the living, with the help of his winged shoes. He was the god of translators and interpreters. Being the most clever of all gods, he served as a messenger for all the others. He also holds in is hand the caduceus, that characteristic wand around which two snakes interlace, which has become today a symbol of doctors and pharmacies, for some.

The planet has a very short revolution around the Sun, 88 terrestrial days, a phenomenon that can explain why in astrology Mercury is so often retrograde. Mercury has, in astrology, attributes similar to the ones found in mythology: before all, communication, intellect, and awareness. Mercury is also about short trips, and transportation in general.

As such, Mercury has become a communicator and protector of travelers, and rules our exchanges and intellect.

We can see these attributes represented as dynamism in Change (18), abundance in Money (19), wit in Intelligence (20), thieves in Theft-Loss (21), commerce in Enterprises (22), travel in Traffic (23), and communication in News (24).

18 - Change

(Changement)

"Make someone or something different; alter or modify. Replace something with something else, especially something of the same kind that is newer or better; substitute one thing for another.
The act or instance of making or becoming different."

Keywords: modification, transformation, evolution, mutation.

The card shows three astrological bodies, which are in order the Earth, the Moon, and the Sun. As all three are aligned on the same axis, with the Moon between the Earth and the Sun, we can see a solar eclipse.

In ancient times, a solar eclipse was universally regarded as something dramatic, a bad omen heralding disaster, as it indicates the concealment of light. At the same time, an eclipse has always been associated with changes, most of the time important, and often more difficult or catastrophic ones.

These days we know that the planets of the Solar system and beyond have a regular and natural movement, well defined by the laws of astronomy. As a result, we are aware now that an eclipse is a natural phenomenon happening quite often, and with regularity. As such, we have to tone down a lot that notion of changes becoming catastrophic.

Change represents modifications, transformations, or an evolution of our projects, everything that is an evolution to our experiences. Change in itself can be good or bad, circumstances around it will indicate in which direction these changes evolve. Of course, being influenced by the Moon, changes always evoke a notion of uncertainty.

As an asset

You are flexible and adapt easily to any situation as it evolves. This allows you to make the required changes beneficial in order to solve your problems. Being nimble is one of the qualities that allows you to move forward.

As a problem

Change can manifest itself in two opposite directions, either a great versatility, or a lack of adaptability. Of course, the context will determine which of these two possibilities is happening in your situation.

You find yourself in a position where you cannot take a stance, or decide on a direction for the course of your actions or your projects. You have a tendency to flip-flop, and as a result constant changes in your your strategies are going to delay the outcome and become problematic.

A lack of adaptability will show itself in difficulties you are having in adapting to your situation and being able to adjust your strategy to circumstances.

As advice

Change evokes the need to evolve, and this is going to require some changes in the way you proceed forward. You must think differently, or act in a different way, or change your strategy, in function of the circumstances surrounding you.

As evolution

Obviously, this card is a harbinger of movement and changes. Moving forward, your situation will evolve, maybe even radically. There will be a significant evolution, moving you in a different direction than what you expected at the beginning.

As outcome

Change indicates that your situation is still in motion, putting you in a position different than the one you started with. As your situation has not reached a stable position, some level of adaptation is required. This is not really something unfavorable, think for instance of a situation that was blocked. In that case, Change might show that what was blocking it has diminished or disappeared.

19 - Money

(Argent)

"Something generally accepted as medium of exchange, a measure of value, or a means of payment."

Keywords: abundance, enrichment, opulence, profusion, wealth, financial success.

On the card we find a cornucopia, mouth downward, filled with coins, that we see pouring out of the horn. The word "cornucopia" is derived from two latin words: "cornu" meaning "horn", and "copia" meaning "plenty". That is certainly why it is referred today as a horn of plenty.

The origin can be traced to the Roman and Greek mythology, where the ornament, shaped like a goat horn, was frequently seen carried by gods and goddesses.

The cornucopia was a symbol of fruitfulness and happiness. Traditionally, it was represented with its mouth upwards, and was the emblem of many deities. With the passage of time, it became and attribute of generosity, prosperity, and good fortune.

On the card, the cornucopia spilling coins symbolizes plenty of money, prosperity and evokes all the possibilities associated with money and wealth. As such, the card bodes well for a financial gain or all material matters.

Money puts an emphasis on the material aspect at the detriment of the spiritual side. But when looking at material aspects, the wealth described can be extended to abundance in any domain.

As an asset

Abundance can of course manifest itself in many different ways and many different domains, but in questions relating to a financial or material matter, Money is a great card to find as an asset, as it will show that you have at your disposal the resources or financial support needed in order to progress toward your goals.

As a problem

You might find yourself in financial trouble or lack the resources necessary to advance your objectives. It is of course easy to extend the context of money to abundance, showing as a consequence that you do not have access to enough means to fix your issues, whatever the domain.

As advice

If would be beneficial for you to look carefully at the financial and material aspects related to your question. Do you have enough wealth or means to move forward? How can you organize your resources the most efficient way to help you with the issues you find on your way?

As evolution

Money highlights all the financial and material

developments that can happen with your projects. But even beyond all this, the card evokes before all the concept of abundance. As such, you see an evolution showing material success, plenty of new things or advantages coming to you.

As outcome

The projects you are involved with are progressing nicely and bringing some form of prosperity, which depending on the domain, could be financial, material, or simply any kind of abundance your project needs.

20 - Intelligence

(Intelligence)

*"The ability to learn or to understand or to deal with new or trying situations.
The ability to apply knowledge to manipulate one's environment or to think abstractly as measured by objective criteria (such as tests).
The act of understanding."*

Keywords: understanding, knowledge, discovering, adaptability, comprehension.

A big book is open, illuminated by a candelabra with seven branches. The book has always been synonymous with knowledge, as paper is the media on which all our comprehension in all the different sciences was recorded.

The candelabra is usually called a menorah, and is used in Jewish worship. In the Middle Ages, it was usually associated with the divine, as it has seven branches symbolizing the seven known planets at that time. The candles are burning and illuminating some pages of the book, a sign that we try to make light on something.

Intelligence, as expressed in the definitions, is what allows us to understand our environment and to reflect on possible directions or actions we can take, or how our mind can help us to deal with our problems or at least try to find solutions to them.

As such, this card represents more our brainpower or intellectual qualities rather than any physical action.

As an asset

As expressed above, Intelligence does not relate to any physical activity, the actions represented by Intelligence are 100% mental. This means that you are using your knowledge and creativity to your advantage, allowing it to find solutions to the problems you are facing.

As a problem

The card could of course mention that your intellectual faculties are limited facing your problems, but much more probable is the fact that you are not using your mental faculties efficiently. This can be reflected in a lack of creativity facing a potential problem, or simply focusing on the wrong aspects of what you are wondering about.

As advice

You should take a step back from acting and take the time to think about how to deal with your situation. Sometimes, the best thing to do when facing some issue, is to take a timeout and reflect on which possibilities or resources could be used to move forward.

It might also be the case when you need to acquire more intellectual skills as you don't have the knowledge required to deal with your situation. Think wisely before acting would be the motto here.

As evolution

The direction your projects are taking allow you to obtain a clearer idea of what is going on, and to apply efficiently your knowledge of the situation. This is a period when openness, and sharing common sense over what can be done is more important than anything else.

As outcome

Intelligence does not predict a positive or negative outcome. As a 100% mental card, it will indicate that you are getting a much better understanding of the situation you are dealing with, allowing you to better adapt yourself to what is going on around you.

21 - Theft - Loss

(Vol - Perte)

*"Theft: the act of dishonestly taking something that belongs to someone else and keeping it.
Loss: the fact that you no longer have something or have less of something."*

Keywords: fear, loss, material worry, breach of trust, negligence, waste of time or resources.

A bat, wings deployed, is grabbing and flying away with a rat, two animals that usually give an impression of not being attractive, even repulsive to many of us.

The bat has always seemed strange with its bastardized aspect: looking like a mouse, but having wings and being capable of flying. In many occidental cultures, the bat was seen as an unclean beast and became a symbol of idolatry and fear. Popular culture and the fact that they are active during the night has made them look like blood-sucking creatures and has associated them with myths such as vampires. A sad representation of a very useful animal, harmless and feeding themselves with insects.

The rat does not have a better reputation. Often seen as unclean and carrier of illnesses, we usually find them close to sewage, garbage, or other unwelcoming places. They have been blamed for spreading diseases, and particularly the bubonic plague that ravaged Europe in the 14th century.

Theft-Loss is thus represented by two animals having a less than respectable reputation, and shows a dual aspect linked to this card. First and foremost, it can show many difficulties, for example a real theft, material disagreements, or someone literally sucking you dry of your energy or resources.

Sometimes also, it can show that we are our own victims, and in this aspect, the card will express things we lose, which can be material, or more subtle ones like wasting time or resources on our endeavors.

As an asset

Some of the cards, like especially this one, do not show any real asset or positive aspect. The best we can expect is that the theft or loss will be limited, or eventually that you are not afraid to commit your time or resources in a way not profitable for you.

As a problem

Theft-Loss can manifest itself in many different ways, showing first material or financial difficulties associated with your projects. It might be because you're wasting your time or resources on what you're working on, or something more nefarious such as being the victim of a real theft. The consequences of this card can effectively be dire, for example people stealing from you financially, materially, or some intellectual property.

As advice

The advice is, of course, not to steal or lose something, but to be on the lookout for such events. You should be careful with whom you associate with and whom you trust, as they could desire something you have. But mostly, you should also look at how you are controlling your resources on a material or financial level, or how you manage your time.

As evolution

The projects you are dealing with are not progressing in a rewarding or profitable way. This can manifest itself in a waste of time or energy, or more generally in your resources diminishing.

Of course, it can also be a literal theft, and you might find yourself surrounded by untrustworthy people, harming the progress of your projects.

As outcome

Someone might have stolen some reward from you and got recognized for some accomplishment in your place. But most probably, this reduction or loss you are seeing is due to your own actions. This can manifest itself in time wasted, or some energy and resources you invested in that do not become profitable. As a result, you are not getting what you expected, and feel like something was taken from you.

22 - Enterprises

(Entreprises)

"A project or undertaking that is especially difficult, complicated, or risky.
A unit of economic organization or activity, like a business organization.
Readiness to engage in daring or difficult action."

Keywords: project, undertake, plan, skills, conception, tools.

The card shows a parchment with a plan drawn on it. There are also several tools present: a hammer behind the parchment, and in front of it a compass and a carpenter square.

These tools refer to freemasonry and companionship, as it was the custom for all French craftsmen to perfect their education by taking a tour around France, doing their apprenticeship before becoming masters of their art.

The compass and the carpenter square refer also to freemasonry, which at the end of the 14th century started to regulate the qualification of stonemasons and their interactions with authorities and clients. Freemasonry and companionship highlight, of course, the skills associated with Enterprises, as we are dealing with masters and craftsmen.

The card evokes all the projects, initiatives, and what we want to undertake in general, with the plan on the parchment being a graphic representation of what we want to build. As such, Enterprises represents our projects in their final stages before realization; what we have committed to do.

An aspect often neglected with this card is rules and regulations associated with what we want to enterprise.

As an asset

Enterprises highlights the qualities that are necessary to realize our projects, such as having the skills and tools necessary to move forward with what we plan to realize. This requires to be able to give structure to our ideas, and having the authorizations and power of organizing things around us.

As a problem

You might lack skills or ideas on how to proceed with your projects, resulting in difficulties to design or start what you are trying to accomplish. You might also lack organization, authorizations, or any other resource needed to start moving forward.

As advice

This is certainly the right time to become more active and proceed to the next step in what you are planning to do. Effectively, you seem to have the mental abilities, material needs, and organizational skills necessary to succeed. All these elements together provide a good opportunity to begin new projects or enhance existing ones, all you need to proceed is to make use of your capabilities of structuring your thoughts and follow a well designed plan.

As evolution

Your projects are well prepared and you take actions to advance to the next phase, allowing them to evolve from planning or an initial phase to a more concrete realization. You can certainly rely on your skills, planning, and organization to move forward in what you want to enterprise.

As outcome

Enterprises does not show a complete realization of your projects, but rather that they evolve and are becoming more concrete. This is certainly a result of your planning, ideas, and actions. As a result, what concerns you evolves toward a satisfactory outcome, and will at some point become reality, unless something really unexpected happens.

Mercury

23 - Traffic

(Trafic)

"The vehicles, pedestrians, ships or planes moving along a route. The volume of customers visiting a business establishment. Import and export trade."

Keywords: travel, exchanges, negotiation, meetings, sales and purchases.

Two snakes are interlaced around a vertical stick, surmounted by a helmet decorated with a pair of wings.

The two intertwining snakes around a stick is the representation of a caduceus. In Greek mythology, the caduceus was the staff carried by Hermes Trismegistus. As we have seen already, Hermes is the Greek version of the Roman god Mercury, who was ruling commerce, and by extension exchanges and communications.

The winged helmet reminds us of Mercury's winged shoes. A helmet is of course an object protecting our head, and as such is frequently seen as a symbol of invulnerability during life. The wings, in addition, represent the ability to fly, and can be seen as a symbol of freedom and spirituality.

Traffic describes any kind of traffic you could encounter. It can be about business, exchange of goods, travel, conversations, etc. At the same time, the helmet and wings will add a notion of being protected in what we exchange.

As a asset

Traffic highlights our dynamism and adaptability. For example how we use these qualities to our advantage when dealing with any situation we find ourselves in. This can be seen as how we can adapt to the elements around us, or change our attitude or position when deemed necessary, or how we are capable of dealing with new adventures.

As a problem

Traffic shows a slowing down and a lack of the flexibility to changes happening around our situation. This can manifest itself in how we are unable to adapt to what is going on, or for instance how inflexible we are when facing changes. Any kind of exchange with others is slowed down or has stopped.

As advice

The card asks you to start acting and not be afraid by all the changes that could happen as a result. Try to adapt yourself to your situation instead of keeping an immovable attitude, it is very important to stay nimble. Your situation is constantly evolving, and you should be ready to correct your stance and your opinions in order to stay on top of what is happening.

As evolution

You can expect an evolution marked with movement,

changes, new happenings, and requiring good communication with others in order to synchronize with them. Your projects might not evolve the way you expected, as you are looking at a kind of evolution where you need to adapt yourself constantly to the situation, making flexibility a key element.

As outcome

Traffic is before all showing a situation which is not final, but still evolving. The card is more about movement, changes, conversations, and as a consequence do not expect a result set in stone.

Of course, if your question was about something that should proceed forward or require some changes, Traffic becomes a good omen that some evolution will happen.

24 - News

(Nouvelle)

*"A report of recent events.
A material reported in a newspaper or news periodical or on a newscast.
What we learn through public rumor, the press, the media.
Opinion that we give or receive."*

Keywords: message, mail, surprise, visit, changes, unexpected events.

The card shows a shooting star, and below it, a bird carrying an envelope.

Shooting stars have always been associated with good luck and happy events. As the tradition goes, when a shooting star appears, it is the right time to make a wish. Shooting stars are also a sign of destiny or divine intervention, and as such they remind us that News is a card influenced by Mercury, the winged god who is a messenger.

Before modern communication systems, birds were often used to carry messages over some distance, as they can travel quickly and quite safely in the sky.

Together with Traffic, these two cards represent extremely well the influence of the Mercury planet; Traffic dealing more with face to face interactions, while News attending more to distance communications and remote events.

It is not surprising in this case that this card is first about news and letters we exchange with others. It can represent any form of communication involving distance. More modern representations of a letter could be expressed by text messages, emails, or any kind of electronic communication.

The other aspect is news as media, often bringing unexpected events, as we are learning about the world around us. This aspect is also relevant if we think about the time period when this oracle was designed, as the only way to learn about the world around us was delivered by the written media.

As an asset

Communicating with others is one of your strengths, you are able to transmit your ideas in a clear way, or to understand quickly the informations you receive. Being well-informed allows you to be flexible enough to adapt yourself quickly to any new event impacting your situation.

As a problem

You have difficulties communicating with others, not capable of expressing clearly your point of view or to understand what others try to communicate. As a result, you lack adaptability and flexibility when faced with unexpected changes and this can hurt you.

As advice

Take the time to put your ideas on paper and share them with others. After all, the main concept of communication is to share information with others. Also, when receiving new information about your projects, you should compare them to what you already know and update your attitude to the new elements.

As evolution

Exchanges with others are good, a well-established and continuous communication with others allows progress to be made. There is also a strong emphasis on novelty, new events you are made aware of, that will lead to opportunities to be seized.

As outcome

As it is the case in the majority of the cards influenced by Mercury, success is not guaranteed with News. What we can expect is that the transmission of information with others is successful, putting you and the other parties involved on the same level. That allows you to fully understand the situation you are in and deal with it.

Venus

Venus is the second planet of the solar system. With a diameter of 7520 miles and a mass about 81.5% of the Earth, Venus is often compared to its orbital neighbor, our planet. It is the third brightest object in the sky, after the Sun and the Moon.

Venus being so bright in the sky, it has always had importance in mythology and astrology thorough history. Venus is named after the Roman goddess of love, fertility, and even prostitution. The divinity was also known by the ancient Greeks as goddess Aphrodite.

However, for the Romans, Venus represented more and particularly Rome's imperial power. Temples were erected in her honor to solicit her assistance in battles.

In astrology, Venus is all about pleasure, and especially

pleasure shared with someone else. It expresses concepts similar to the ones found in mythology, first of all love, romance, and harmony in our relationships. Venus is also about spreading happiness, appreciating others and the things we possess. Beauty, the arts, and aesthetics are also aspects related to Venus.

As such, Venus represents first love, beauty, aesthetics, grace, and pleasure. Being a goddess of love and beauty, it also makes sense that the planet is seen as a representation of women in general and femininity.

By extension, Venus has always represented the arts, whatever their form, and artists. For example, we can see an expression of the arts and beauty in the Venus de Milo, often seen as representing an ideal of feminine beauty.

With all these qualities, Venus can express itself in Pleasure (25) as all kinds of pleasurable activities, in Peace (26) as harmony and balance, in Union (27) and Family (28) as love and wellbeing, in Amor (29) as love and grace, in The Table (30) as pleasure, and in Passions (31) as pleasure and beauty.

25 - Pleasures

(Plaisirs)

"A feeling of enjoyment or satisfaction, or something that produces this feeling."

Keywords: Joy, contentment, bliss, amusement, being artistic, artistic pleasure.

In the middle of the card we see a lyre, a musical instrument which was mostly used during antiquity. The lyre is the ancestor of the harp, and was accompanying the muses, nine Greco-Roman deities who inspired all forms of art.

As a consequence, Pleasures resonates well with these activities, the satisfaction and all the happy feelings we can get through our five senses: what we see, hear, feel, taste, and smell. Arts and the beauty they deliver are certainly the biggest part of what this card can signify.

Pleasure also puts forward warm feelings such as joy and entertainment. It expresses the need to have fun and being surrounded by happy activities.

Pleasures is very similar to card (45) Happiness. The main difference being the influence of the planet. Venus gives a notion of immediate satisfaction, pleasure and joy, while the Jupiter influence in Happiness is more about expansion, and as a consequence something that will last longer.

As an asset

You find yourself in very good dispositions to work on your projects. Effectively, feelings such as optimism, joy and amusement rule your emotions, giving you a boost in how you see your situation and how deal with it. You are ready to attack your problems with a feeling of joy and pleasure.

As a problem

You have difficulties to find any pleasure or satisfaction in what relates to your questions or the situation you find yourself in. You are probably not in a position where you can flourish and take advantage of what is happening around you. As a consequence, the problem is not really that you cannot do something about your issues, but rather that you find no joy in doing it and your well-being is put into question.

As advice

First of all, find pleasure in what you're doing. Your attitude facing a problem does not have to be serious, you would be better served by trying to find the positive aspects of what you are dealing with. You must think first about yourself, and all your choices should be done in a way that would give you some pleasure first.

As evolution

Your projects are evolving in a pleasant manner, giving you a lot of contentment. Everything is moving forward steadily, the emphasis is more in finding personal satisfaction, maybe more by moving slowly toward a conclusion if that way to proceed gives you joy, rather than a drastic movement forward but less pleasant.

As outcome

Same as how your projects are evolving, the outcome does not show something drastic coming. So, you should not expect a huge step forward in the accomplishment of your goals. The emphasis is more in feeling satisfied and happy with what your projects become, even if not reaching a complete resolution.

26 - Peace

(La Paix)

*"Freedom from war and violence, especially when people live and work together happily without disagreement.
The state of not being interrupted or annoyed with worry, problems, noise, or unwanted actions."*

Keywords: reconciliation, agreement, appeasement, tranquility.

    A double-edge axe is surrounded by a bound bundle of wooden rods. Below it, there is a crown of laurels. The laurels are, as seen earlier with Success, a symbol of victory, honor, and peace.
    The axe shown on this card is a fasces, a symbol having its origin in the Etruscan civilization. In ancient Rome, it symbolized a Roman king's power to punish his subjects. It was held by a lictor, an officer attending a consul or magistrate, and executing sentences on offenders. Later, it became a symbol of a magistrate's power and jurisdiction. During the first half of the 20th century, the fasces became

heavily identified with the fascism movements.

If we look at where the oracle Belline originated, France, and at the time of Mage Edmond, roughly half a century after the French Revolution, the fasces represented a symbol showing that the power belonged to the people. It also symbolizes the unity and indivisibility of the Republic, as stated in the French constitution.

The card relates to a serene situation, one where an agreement between parties seems to have been reached. The influence of Venus adds a feeling of serenity and well-being, in which conflict can be avoided. Peace can also express that a stable and peaceful situation has been established.

Of course, there is no indication on how that peaceful atmosphere is obtained. It might be because of an agreement between the parties, by respect of established laws and customs, or by fear of a punishment.

As an asset

You are able to negotiate the avoidance of conflict and find an agreement for the situation you are involved with. That allows you the possibility to act in the events happening before you and easily find a compromise. You put forward your sense of negotiation first, as you are looking mostly to find harmony and agreement.

As a problem

Depending on your question, we can see this card evoking with two different possibilities.

It might be that you want a peaceful resolution when a more drastic action is necessary, like for instance you are staying passive and peaceful instead of fighting for what you want.

But more probably, there is a lack of agreement. Conflicts

and disputes abound with other people involved, to the point where you are not capable of finding any agreement with them.

As advice

Peace invites you to, as the expression says, 'bury the hatchet' and calm things down. Instead of a difficult advancement or bitter defeat, it is better to look for a compromise, in order to be able to unblock your conflictual situation and move forward.

As evolution

Nothing conflictual or particularly difficult seems to emerge, allowing your projects to move in a tranquil direction. Your situation remains quiet, everything moves forward without many difficulties or disputes, a pleasant and calm atmosphere prevails.

As outcome

Peace guarantees a pleasant and peaceful result, but it does not mean that you will find satisfaction in the outcome. If, for instance, your question is about finding victory or any advantage over something, Peace does not promise that you will get it, Peace is more about finding a compromise or a result that will be agreeable to all the parties involved.

27 - Union

(Union)

"An act or instance of uniting or joining two or more things into one such as a uniting in marriage."

Keywords: commitment, love, marriage, promise, availability.

A golden altar is decorated with a ribbon of pearls and flowers. On top of it, two hearts are suspended and surrounded by flames.

The hearts have always been a symbol used to represent our emotions, especially affection and love. Effectively, a heart is often found in drawings and emojis to represent romantic feelings, and two hearts beating together will represent two amorous partners. The flames surrounding these hearts add a notion of something burning, a symbolic representation of the passion or intense love between the partners.

An altar has always been a place where we consecrate things or events, and of course in this particular case, it is used to consecrate the love of these two beating hearts.

If we add to these elements the influence of the planet, Venus, Union first represents love, and more directly our commitment to it.

As a consequence, we can see two people joined together when this card comes up, and all kinds of partnerships. It can be marriage, love, friendship, feelings between people, or even all the partnerships we establish in life, like in business for instance. What is important with Union, is that the partnership, whatever is is, is made official and public.

By extension, the card can also represent all the situations where we join two things together, publicly.

As an asset

Union shows that you can easily form beneficial associations with others having similar goals if that helps you to reach your objectives more easily. In this way, contact with others helps you to flourish, demonstrating how a partnership can be conducive to the pursuit of a common goal.

As a problem

Partnerships are difficult to establish, or established ones are not reliable and difficult to maintain. This might be due to difficulties to communicate between the parties, or to disagree on the common goals or how to reach them. Whatever the reason, this will hurt the possibility to reach your objectives.

As advice

With Union, it becomes important to find people who can help you to achieve your goals. You might even want to form some kind of temporary association or partnership if it proves to be the best way for you to move forward.

In romantic situations, Union would advise you to declare your flame for the other and show your willingness to engage in the next step of the relationship, making the relation formal if it is not yet, or even proposing a higher level of commitment.

As evolution

An association with others allows both parties to move forward toward a common goal, and as such the partnership evokes a favorable direction for the situation you find yourself in.

Of course, if your question is about a romantic situation, Union is extremely advantageous for the evolution of your situation, as it might indicate a more serious engagement between the partners.

As outcome

Union will mostly appear when a particular situation results in a partnership or association with others. In business, it might be joining forces with someone else, or two companies working together.

Union will often appear in romantic situations and forecasts a very satisfying outcome, where romantic feelings prevail, to the point of establishing some form of commitment between the partners, or even marriage.

28 - Family

(Famille)

*"A group of people who are related to each other, such as a mother, a father, and their children.
A group of people who care about each other because they have a close relationship or shared interests."*

Keywords: family, close friendship, trusted association, group, shared interests.

    A hen is taking care of its five chicks. Like a good mother, the bird is watching over its offspring and feeding them. Something remarkable on the image is that the hen has its wings deployed over the flock, a sign of protection from the environment around them.
    From this simple image, it is quite easy to deduct what this card influenced by Venus is about. Family, by definition, means people who are blood related, but by extension, we can consider in the spirit of this card any kind of group or association where people have a common goal or shared interest. Through that optic, any group of people having

anything in common between them can be considered.

As an asset

Relations in general are important to you and forming bonds with others come easily. As a result, you have no difficulty to form a support system or alliances built around people that trust you and can help you to achieve your goals. You are a natural born leader who can organize and lead people.

As a problem

There could be two different types of problems with this card.

Either you have difficulties to establish associations or bonds with other people, and you are left alone without any support to try to resolve your issues.

Or your bonds with others are too close and personal when it would be beneficial to act alone, hurting your chances of moving forward in your projects.

Whatever the case, Family shows that there is a problem related to partnerships with others.

As advice

Family indicates that it would be beneficial for you to rely on others and establish some kind of contact or relation with them. It might be people you are related to or others that you trust. What is important is to find people having the same ideas and create bonds with them, as cooperation will allow some shared goals to be reached more easily.

As evolution

Family forecasts a favorable evolution if your question is about relations with others, on any level. Bonds start forming between the different partners and trust in each other becomes prevalent. Getting support from others and being able to rely on them allows a for a smooth evolution toward a nice resolution of the issues.

As outcome
There has been a favorable climate for the development of solid friendships, bonds, or associations between all the people involved in the situation. As a result, Family bodes well if your question relates to any kind of relationship or human interaction. In other cases, Family will indicate that you can count on the support of others, even if the outcome is not 100% favorable.

29 - Love

(Amor)

*"The ancient Roman god of love; Cupid.
In medieval literature, a romantic ideal defined in opposition to the union or marriage and where veneration of the lady leads the knight to surpass himself to sublimate his desire."*

Keywords: love, happiness, feelings, pleasure, relationship.

Two hearts are placed together and surrounded by a garland made of flowers. Below it a dove, with wings deployed, seems to take flight.

The dove is a universal symbol of peace, spirituality, hope, and love. From the two hearts, flames are burning on top, representing the passion that links them. The garland of flowers adds a notion of happiness and beauty to that picture, an analogy for blooming love.

This is the second of three cards, in the series related to Venus, showing two hearts. But in contrary to the first one, Union (27), here the two hearts are not suspended in flames, the flames are smaller and on top.

There is a big difference between a union, or marriage, and love. While the former represents a partnership, the latter, with these two hearts, is more about a representation of feelings. In this card, love is also pure, as shown by the dove. Another big difference with Union is that it represents an official act and as such is public, while the love expressed on this card could be public or private.

Love, of course, announces a meeting of people, new relationships between two persons, new romantic feelings growing. And of course, if the question does not relate to romance, the card can represent a platonic love, like the one we would have for our job or something else important in our life.

As an asset

Love represents a situation where people involved feel warm and generous. This attitude gives you the capacity and charm required to seduce others and rally them to your cause. The bond you create with them might be weaker than the one represented in Union (27), but the feelings will still be strong and pure.

As a problem

There is a lack of affection, you are not appreciated to your just value, hindering your chances of reaching your objectives. People are cold around you and do not recognize your value. If your question concerns a romantic relationship, no feelings are developing between you, probably leading to a disappointment.

As advice

As the main energy of the card is about love, you should use your charm to your advantage. So, be charming, loving, generous with others, show that you care for them. Try to establish good contact with others that can help you in reaching your objectives. If the question is about a romantic relationship, do not hesitate to show your feelings and tell the other that you care about them.

As evolution

You can see a pleasant evolution in your projects, where respect with others involved is mutual. If your question concerns a relationship, you can expect that feelings for each other are reciprocated and will grow.

As outcome

Love is all around, and the card predicts a lot of satisfaction, resulting in a positive increase in the way you feel. You can expect great satisfaction for your projects, undoubtedly more on a spiritual level than material. If you are involved in a relationship, expect that love to flourish.

30 - The Table

(La Table)

"A piece of furniture with a flat top and one or more legs, providing a level surface on which objects may be placed, and that can be used for such purposes as eating, writing, working, or playing games."

Keywords: conviviality, pleasure, entertainment, sharing, celebration.

On the image we find one amphora and two cups. An amphora is an ancient Greek or Roman two-handled jar, usually made of ceramic, and was used for the storage or transport of various products both liquid and solid, mostly wine, oil, milk, or grain. Cups are of course used to contain liquid and to drink. Symbolically they are often associated with emotions and celebrations. As is often the practice, raising your cup to someone means celebrating that person.

With all these elements, and the influence of Venus, we can safely deduce that the main usage depicted on the card is certainly to sit, symbolically offer wine, and celebrate with others.

In that context, The Table makes reference to meals and moments we share with others, when we have the possibility to share not only a good drink or food, but also discussions and our different life experiences.

As such, The Table will show these moments when we share conviviality with others, celebrations with friends or family. By extension, it can also indicate meetings and gatherings with others, such as work meetings or group encounters for example.

As an asset

You rely on your sense of hospitality and conviviality to establish contact with others. These qualities allow you to develop relations and establish solid links with others, or to easily express your ideas and reach some following in order to develop your projects.

As a problem

As a problem, your lack of conviviality and your difficulties to convince others make it almost impossible for you to establish meaningful contacts. All that inertia and absence of support leaves you alone to deal with your problems and hurts your chances of solving them.

As advice

You should try to involve yourself more with others. Invite them for a drink, or simply sit with them and have a discussion about your issues. Often a good conversation with friends or associates will help develop leads allowing you to move forward toward a resolution of your conflicts.

As evolution

By itself, the Table does not show much evolution for your projects if they relate to actions more concrete than dealing with relations with others. As the symbolism of the card indicates, the evolution will mostly be marked by how pleasurable you find your situation and how you are making new friendships and establishing important contacts.

As outcome

Same as for the evolution of your situation, the Table, while it is still a possibility, does not really indicate a successful completion of your projects. The card highlights more an attitude of sharing with others and conviviality. What is really important to remember, is that even if your goals are not completely reached, contentment with new friendships or contacts has become more important.

31 - Passions

(Passions)

*"A very powerful feeling, for example or sexual attraction, love, hate, anger, or other emotion.
A strong or extravagant fondness, enthusiasm, or desire for anything."*

Keywords: ardor, irrational love, desire, attraction.

This is the third card in the series influenced by Venus showing two hearts. At the bottom there is a rooster, and above him, two hearts, each with a small flame on top, and pierced by an arrow.

The rooster is often presented as the master of the farmyard, and oftentimes aggressive. On the image, crest up, in an expression of hostility, it seems to control what is around. Effectively, roosters are very territorial, not allowing another one to come close.

The two pierced hearts remind us of Cupid and his bow and how love and passion can hit us at any moment, and light that flame representing a fiery comportment. The arrows and the flames point in different directions, showing how immature and unpredictable our feelings for others can be.

As opposed to the two preceding cards showing two hearts, the mood on this one is more agitated. Passions are often expressed by very strong emotions, most of the time even dominating our reason.

As a result, adding to these hearts the aggressiveness of the rooster, the feelings expressed in this card are very strong, showing a lot of ardor. Passions evokes very intense emotions, much less controlled than in Union (27) or Love (29), something having not yet reached any form of stability.

Passions evoke something different than having feelings for someone else, as we can be passionate about many different activities or hobbies.

As an asset

Have you even seen someone talking about their passions? Being passionate for someone or something usually gives you wings, allowing you to explore and and create what is needed without fear and being held back. These strong emotions and desire to succeed bring you to a position where your attitude allows you to do what is necessary to further your cause.

As a problem

Passions, together with the immature feelings it brings, can compromise your goals. You are effectively prone to intense, but selfish desires that usually do not last, as your passion for what you are doing wanes quickly. The resulting danger is that what attracts you today might not last long enough to accomplish what you want to realize.

In relationships, that immaturity, even if intense feelings

exist, is often responsible for disputes, a warning that a reconciliation is sometimes difficult.

As advice

Being passionate for someone or something will give you the strength to trust yourself and act in a spontaneous way. Basically, you find yourself in a very emotional situation, and are capable of benefiting from where your feelings will lead you. Thus, you should not let your reason dictate your actions, your can trust your instincts.

As evolution

Your projects evolve in a direction that gives you great pleasure. What is happening around you gives birth to extreme feelings, leading to very strong emotions that will help you to feel more involved in your situation.

As outcome

A lot of pleasurable and positive emotions are linked to this card, and as a result success for your endeavors is certainly a real possibility. The only problem, as seen above, is that when passion dominates, what is happening reaches a high point and the resulting feelings usually are short lived, then slowly diminish. In that aspect, the success obtained might not last if you are not careful.

Mars

Mars is the fourth planet from the Sun, and the last terrestrial one. It is nicknamed "the red planet" because of the reddish color of its surface, due to finely grained iron oxide dust in the soil.

Mars is among the brightest celestial objects, it looks like a bright red point of light, and has been known since ancient times.

The planet is named after the Roman god of war, who was second in importance to Jupiter. In Roman literature, he was protector of Rome. Early Romans revered Mars as a raging god, whose fury inspired the savagery of warfare. Mars was largely based on the Greek god Ares, the god of war, and shares much of the same mythology.

In symbology, the symbol representing Mars consists of

a round and a spear, and is also known as the sign for "maleness".

Mars is the planet of action in astrology. Some aspects of your life controlled by Mars include your passions, determination, drive, and energy. And while Venus controls romantic attraction, Mars rules over your sexual energy and desire. It has also a nefarious aspect, predicting conflicts and catastrophes.

If we take into account all these aspects taken in association with its red color, we get a feeling synonymous with aggression, ambition, and bravery. Do not expect a quiet moment with Mars, a lot of energy will certainly be spent when Mars is present.

As such, it is not surprising to find difficult cards under the influence of this planet. Mars expresses itself as a passive aggression in Meanness (32), conflicting ideas in Trial (33), crushing others in Despotism (34), aggression is Enemies (35), rough talks in Negotiations (36), aggressiveness in Fire (37), and catastrophic events in Accident (38).

32 - Meanness

(Méchanceté)

*"The quality of being unwilling to give or share things.
The quality of being unkind towards other people.
The desire to cause pain for the satisfaction of doing harm."*

Keywords: selfishness, cruelty, vice, unkindness, treason.

On the card, we find a lantern and a knife hidden behind it, on the darker side.

In popular folklore, a lantern does not have a good reputation. This is probably due to the fact that it does not provide much light, not enough to see clearly around us when the night is dark. Here we probably have a "dark lantern", one with a sliding shutter allowing to make it dark without extinguishing the candle. It allowed thieves and bandits the possibility to stay hidden until their prey approached them.

The knife is a weapon, something used to threaten, attack, or defend oneself. By analogy it can represent an aggressive and brutal attitude, one where someone wants to hurt another being not only physically, but also on the mental plane. On the card, the knife is hidden by the lantern, adding a climate of falsehood and hiding someone's intentions in order to hurt another being.

With all these elements taken together, Meanness is foremost about violence, mostly a psychological one. It is therefore the moral values which are attacked by this card. It represents an atmosphere of nuisance, in which the consultant must be vigilant.

As an asset

First, you can use the qualities of the card to your own advantage. By this, I do not mean you to be aggressive or cruel, but rather to use the lantern to shed light on what is not clear around you, and to be armed with a weapon to defend yourself, mostly against cruelty and moral attacks.

It can also mean that you can gain some kind of advantage by applying pressure on someone else, like for instance reminding someone that they owe you something or shining light on some aspect they would like to keep hidden.

As a problem

The climate surrounding you is certainly not auspicious to be able to move your projects forward. You can expect to find yourself in situations where you cannot trust other people involved. It is more a climate where each one fights for their own advantage. This can harm your objectives, as some others are ready to use unkind or unlawful tactics to gain some advantage over you.

As advice

Be careful with whom you associate and who you can

trust. If you find yourself in a difficult situation, you should be ready to defend yourself. The knife is a weapon at your disposal, do not hesitate to show it or threaten others that you will use it if they try to abuse you.

As evolution

The evolution of your projects is not going to be easy nor straightforward, there are many possible disruptions due to external influences due to unkind attitudes. Your situation can become complicated if you do not act carefully, or if you are too confident in other persons involved.

As outcome

Meanness shows that difficulties will be found when trying to realize your objectives. The problems are not due to the way you act or the actions you take to reach your goals, but from the climate surrounding you, and the fact that you cannot trust anybody around you. As a result, you have to constantly deal with their aggressiveness and treasonous attitude.

33 - Trial

(Procès)

"The hearing of statements and showing of objects, etc. in a law court to judge if a person is guilty of a crime or to decide a case or legal matter.
To test something in a formal way to discover how effective or suitable it is."

Keywords: conflict, opposition, antagonism, dispute, debate.

Two swords are crossed, a sign that they are engaging in a duel or any kind of combative exercise. A sword is a weapon, something someone would use to attack or defend themselves, and as a result they usually symbolize qualities such as power, protection, might, authority, courage, antagonism.

Trial, of course, by its name reminds us of tribunals and how justice is delivered. The decisions taken there are important and often difficult for at least one of the parties. As such, Trial can represent the legal system and judiciary problems you might face, but also debates, opposing arguments, as well as decisions taken and their consequences.

On the card, the two swords are crossed, indicating a clash between opponents, which can be symbolically a sign of opposing or conflicting ideas, or a difficult choice that must be made. Let's not forget that swords are also symbols of battles and war. By extension, Trial can represent antagonism, fights, disputes and even violence.

As an asset

As swords are weapons, you have the means to defend yourself and attack if necessary. As a consequence, justice is on your side as you are capable of presenting arguments in your favor.

As swords cut, you are also capable of sharp decisions, which allows you, through debates or discussions, to negotiate your point of view skillfully and to find compromises that work in your favor.

As a problem

You find yourself in a position of weakness because your debating skills and your arguments are not very effective. This can manifest itself in taking wrong decisions, arguing for a lost cause, or facing a difficult situation for which you cannot reach a compromise, leaving you in a grueling position.

As advice

You must be ready to face your adversaries and fight to advance your ideas, meaning that you must take a clear and firm position, devoid of ambiguity. Be ready to face an open conflict and react in a violent way, sometimes the only possibility for advancing is to wage war on your adversaries.

As evolution

You will find yourself facing some conflicts and the need to arbitrate several situations, some of them might even be very antagonistic. This will require for you to fight and assert your rights in front of others.

As outcome

Trial, by definition, is all about conflicts, discussions, and some points that need to be resolved. As a consequence, it cannot show a clear success or failure for your projects, but rather a continuing situation where you have to defend yourself with constant arguments and conflicts.

34 - Despotism

(Despotisme)

"The exercise of absolute power, specially in a cruel and oppressive way.
A country or political system where the ruler holds absolute power."

Keywords: authority, inability to act, submission, resignation, passivity.

    To fully understand Despotism, we must go back to the definition of the word, which is foremost a political system where one person has absolute power. It defines a totalitarian regime, under which freedom is deprived from all the persons living under the authority of the tyrant. As a result, there is a feeling of being completely humiliated and dominated in this card.
    The image represents very well these notions. We see a man with his wrists chained to a stake. Almost naked, head bent, with an attitude of resignation, we can easily imagine that this man is deprived of his freedom, subjected to a

strong authority against which he can do absolutely nothing.

With his hands tied, powerless in a position of victim, there is nothing he can do to escape his condition, and he seems determined to accept his fate, unable to rebel.

Despotism indicates a pattern of behaviors. It announces first a period in the life of the consultant when all his power has been removed, and he is no longer allowed to make decisions by himself. He has become a spectator of his life and is not capable of taking action to change his condition.

As a result, the card warns of inaction, the dangers of resignation and accepting one's condition without taking action to change it.

As an asset

There is nothing much favorable about this card, the best you can do, as long as the situation is not evolving, is to wait patiently until days become better.

You find the time to fly under the radar, and quietly hide your intentions.

As a problem

We can see this card under two different aspects, either you are the tyrant, or the person under tyranny.

In the first case, your authority is not respected, and you can expect other people involved in your situation to revolt, and to do everything in their power to block your actions.

In the second case, you suffer a great domination, which can be due to other people or the elements surrounding your situation. As such, you are not capable to act and progress toward your goals.

As advice

As by definition despotism is submitting yourself to the authority of forces beyond your control. Your only chance is not acting, of doing nothing because action would work against you. All you can do is to wait patiently until you feel liberated and your situation improves. In the meantime, the only thing you can do is think about your situation and make plans for later.

As evolution

Your project is like that person repressed and chained; under external forces on which you do not have power to act. That leaves you no room to maneuver or act on your own. Caution is advised as the progression of your projects does not depend on you, but on the actions of others.

As outcome

You find yourself in a position where outside forces control your destiny, and you have no decision-making power over the success or failure of your plans. All you can do is wait patiently for your situation to improve and accept what is happening around you. Despotism certainly indicates that you should greatly lower your expectations.

35 - Enemies

(Ennemis)

*"A person who hates or opposes another person and tries to harm them or stop them from doing something.
A country, or the armed forces of a country, that is at war with another country.
A thing that harms or weakens something else."*

Keywords: hostility, malevolence, significant difficulties, adversity, competition, malice.

The picture shows a snake wrapped around a sword. A blade is a weapon and is used to cut, to attack and defend oneself. Cutting can go beyond a physical action and symbolically represent words that cut; a sharp tongue.

Surrounded by the snake, which can represent treason, lies, or calumnies, we can imagine an unhealthy situation. The serpent points its head above the blade, we can see its tongue. It is ready to attack and deliver its venom.

Being under the influence of Mars, Enemies defines first someone who seeks to harm someone else. And on this card, the word enemies is plural, indicating that there may be several sources of harm. In this context, the card can represent the querent facing people that could hurt them, lie or put them in unpleasant and difficult situations.

If we go beyond the literal, and look at a more symbolic interpretation, the snake can represent not only people, but also all kinds of tricky situations where obstacles will be in the way of the querent. They can slow them down, or hurt him by constantly having to check the veracity of the circumstances surrounding them.

The tongue of the snake can also makes us think of popular expressions, among others scandalmongering. The querent should be careful of what kind of rumors and malicious gossip is spilled around them. Together with the sharpness of the blade, these rumors can be vicious and can really cause trouble.

As an asset

In this case, we could consider the querent as being the one holding the sword, and being capable of defending their position. Facing adversity, you know you can fight back and find a way to get yourself out of the difficult or calumnious situations you find yourself involved in.

As a problem

You find yourself facing important difficulties, as some people oppose you or lie to you. The situation you find yourself in is not favorable for you in order to move forward, as you have to constantly check your environment to detect the malicious intents of other people involved.

As advice

As you are surrounded by problems that you should not take lightly, you should not confide too much in your associates or persons closely in contact with you. Be careful in how you act with people around you, and while you do not want to exacerbate the aggressive climate you find yourself in, be on the lookout for lies and falsehoods.

As evolution

You should expect adversity and disagreements, as some powerful forces are evolving against you. Whatever the context, Enemies shows a very difficult evolution in which you will have to move carefully, as you find yourself in a situation filled with lies, hurtful intents, and strong opposition to your projects.

As outcome

You will face inconveniences and contradictions that will end up causing trouble. These will be revealed as conflicts, unfriendly situations. As such, do not expect a resolution of your problems, but more a continuity of the same or worsening circumstances, where you constantly have to check who you can trust or not, and a constant adversarial climate.

36 - Negotiations

(Pourparlers)

"The process of discussing something with someone in order to reach an agreement with them, or the discussions themselves. A formal discussion between people who are trying to reach an agreement."

Keywords: discussions, debate, exchange, diplomacy, gossip.

A flock of three birds perched on a bare tree is joined by a fourth. All of them have an open beak, suggesting sounds. If you observe birds and their behavior, they are really well in the spirit of the Mars energy. Birds on a branch, or close together, are very nervous, constantly moving, singing, often upsetting and even attacking each other, and ready to fly away at the first sign of a larger conflict.

Looking at the birds, they all seem to babble at the same time, giving an impression of cacophony. Symbolically, this can represent talks, conversations, discussions, that we have with others.

In an ideal debate, we would each take our turn to talk and defend our arguments, then reciprocate the same courtesy to others. But this is not the impression we get from the situation depicted on this card. Here the combative and even aggressive attitudes linked to the ruling planet, Mars, seem well-represented.

Negotiations can represent a wide range of different attitudes, going from the respectful conversations we have with someone else, up to completely animated discussions where each one of the speakers tries to dominate the others.

A negotiation happens when there is a conflict or difference of opinion, and each one of the parties involved tries to express their opinion and point of view in order to find common ground. And of course during these negotiations, tensions can run high and the arguments can be vigorously defended.

As an asset

You have the skills of a good debater, and you can express your opinion with energy, passion, and conviction. You are also capable of leading a debate and direct it in a way that will find a compromise in your favor.

As a problem

Negotiations can be seen as a warning that you are too combative and aggressive in the way you try to defend your opinions. Your might turn people against you with the arguments you put forward, and how you want to dominate the discussions.

As advice

Before taking any further action, you might want to prioritize talks and communications with others to try to solve contentious points. Dialogue should always prevail before taking more drastic actions. Try to motivate others to reach a consensus, by having a constructive debate.

As evolution

Expect a lot of discussions and uncertainties due to the fact that no resolution of the current issues is coming anytime soon. The debate drags on forever, no one agrees and a consensus is very difficult to reach. As a result, not much evolution seems to happen to your projects, as they constantly face some questioning.

As outcome

As was hinted in the evolution of your projects, there is no real resolution. Some points remain in contention and are still up for debate. Do not expect any fast settlement, as some opposition remains. At best Negotiations can indicate some friendly talks about remaining issues that will lead to a temporary truce.

37 - Fire

(Feu)

"Combusting or burning, in which substances combine chemically with oxygen from the air and typically give out bright light, heat, and smoke.
The shooting of guns or other weapons.
Strong emotion."

Keywords: dynamism, drive, determination, strength, will, fight.

Two roosters seem ready to fight, there is a torch burning on top of them. The attitude of the two birds is decidedly aggressive, each with one leg up, head down and facing each other. Contact is imminent, there's nothing to restrain them. All they show are feelings of combativeness, fearlessness, and determination. Their attitude leaves no room for doubt or fear.

The name of the card refers to one of the four basic elements of matter, as already defined by the ancient Greeks: fire, water, air, and earth. The idea that these four elements made up all matter was the cornerstone of philosophy, science, and medicine. Fire typically represents our passions, desires, survival, but also more nefarious attributes such as anger, fight, primal instincts.

Historically, fire was very important. Going back to the prehistoric times, it allowed our ancestors to see in the dark, defend themselves, cook and heat their space.

All these aspects can be linked together to show the aggressiveness and determination we see in this card. It seems that these two roosters are ready to fight until death. In a farmyard, only one rooster is generally present, as putting two together will result in fights over which one is the king of the hens.

As such, the card can certainly represent our primal instincts, what makes us tick. Fire symbolizes fight, struggle, our dynamism to win.

As an asset

You are strong and have enough stamina to impose your will on others and obtain what you are looking for. Fire burns in you, and like in the farmyard, you are the one that remains in power.

As a problem

We see two harmful attitudes with this card.

Either your aggressiveness is not helping your cause, and your constant combative attitude is not helping you gain support. Instead, expect others involved in your situation to rebel.

Or, you don't have enough fire in you to fight for what you want. This causes you to be overwhelmed by the attitude and will of others around you, putting you in a dire situation and threatening your goals.

As advice

Fire advises you to fight in order to obtain what you desire. You should harness the energy and strength that burn in you in order to be more vigorous in the way you move forward. Assert yourself, and even if that means that you have to endure direct hits or reproaches, you must channel all your energy, as you should act with firmness and determination.

As evolution

Moving your goals forward is not going to be simple, as you can expect resistance from the other parties involved. You will have to deal with adversity and struggles. But you have no choice; if you want your project to evolve, you will have to fight to obtain what you want.

As outcome

Fire evokes continuous fights and struggle, so there is no end to conflicts and opposition to your objectives. As a result, expect that you will be facing some opponent or an unfavorable situation. The best outcome you can expect, is to constantly fight for what you want, or risk losing it.

38 - Accident

(Accident)

"A unfortunate incident that happens unexpectedly and unintentionally, typically resulting in damage or injury. An event that happens by chance or that is without apparent or deliberate cause."

Keywords: unforeseen events, change, unexpected modification, collapse, destruction.

Two towers are struck by lightning and are collapsing. A lightning bolt traditionally represents a sudden illumination and the destruction of ignorance. It can also represent the "wrath of God", a punishment of humans by the Gods, coming from the sky. The tower, of course, is a man-made construction, which is not eternal.

The message is simple: sometimes our beliefs, our foundations and their bases are struck down when we do not expect it. Accidents and unforeseen circumstances can happen at any moment and have a strong and lasting impact on us.

But even if the crisis can be strong, the presence of greenery at the bottom of the towers is a sign that life always grows back, a reason to keep some hope even in the worst of times, as we can bounce back from unforeseen and disastrous circumstances.

Accident reminds us of all these occasions when things don't go our way, when we feel completely down because of what is destroyed in our lives. As a consequence, we will have to face unforeseen circumstances and adapt to them.

Accident can also warn us to be careful, the card can mean a real accident, literally.

As an asset

You have a great facility to adapt to the circumstances surrounding you. Sometimes, brutal changes of direction are necessary in order to pursue your goals, changes that require extensive rework of what you are doing, and you are capable to execute them easily. Flexibility to adapt to the events around you is an asset you master.

As a problem

Nothing is going your way, you can expect difficulties, burdens, and sudden actions that will go against your goals. The only thing you can do is take note of what went wrong and try to adapt to the circumstances. Accident can also mean that luck is not on your side, unexpected turns of events are playing against you, or at least slowing you down.

As advice

Be careful to not take too many risks, you should question your decisions and rethink your position as your projects might be headed into a very dangerous situation. As a result some radical action might be necessary, such as totally changing what was already done, and trying to reach your goals in a totally different, less risk-prone direction.

As evolution

Expect a difficult evolution for your projects. Be careful, the direction taken by your actions can reveal itself dangerous and lead you to a very difficult position, or to your actions imploding. The way you are trying to reach your goals will not succeed, it will be necessary for you to try to reach them by restarting differently, probably from scratch.

As outcome

Success is not coming, some setback happened. Contrary to your expectations, your goals will not be met, probably due to something drastic and unexpected, and you will have to question what happened. At that point, just like when you are caught in a real accident, the only thing you can do is try to understand what happened and how your expectations could not be met.

Jupiter

Jupiter is the fifth planet of the solar system and the largest. Jupiter has been known since ancient times as it is visible to the naked eye. It is usually associated to the Greek god Zeus, or the Roman equivalent of Jupiter.

Jupiter, also known as Jove, was the god of sky and thunder, as well as the king of the gods in ancient Roman mythology. He was the top god of the Roman pantheon, and considered the chief deity of Roman state religion during the Republican and Imperial eras, until Christianity became the main religion.

In astrology, Jupiter is the thinking person's planet, using higher learning, giving us the gift of exploring ideas, the intellect and spirituality. In the more spiritual realm, Jupiter rules over religion and philosophy.

Luck and good fortune are usually associated with Jupiter, a planet allowing us growth and to flourish in a positive way.

It is no wonder then that these qualities can be seen quite favorably in the seven cards ruled by this planet. Support (39) refers to the help we're getting from our community. Beauty (40) refers to the notions of exploring and expanding our knowledge. Heritage (41) talks about our experience coming from our interactions with others. Wisdom (42) refers directly to the experience we're getting with the intellectual aspects. Fame (43) refers to the recognition of our actions. Hazard (44) shows how we are evolving our explorations. Happiness (45) refers directly to our social recognition.

Jupiter

39 - Support

(Appui)

*"To agree with and give encouragement to someone or something because you want him, her, or it to succeed.
To endure bravely or quietly.
To hold up or or serve as a foundation or prop for."*

Keywords: help, assistance, support, solid foundations, kindness.

    An eagle, wings outstretched, stands on a golden globe and is wearing a crown. Its posture shows that he is ready to take flight, in full control. He's looking to the right, a direction which symbolically represents the future.
    Historically, eagles have always be seen as the more majestic of the birds. As they roam the skies, they were believed to have a special communication with the gods. They have always represented pride, majesty, strength, courage, and wisdom. Their image is often adopted as a symbol by countries, armies or powerful organizations.
    Symbolically, when an eagle appears, it means that you

are being put on notice to be inspired and push yourself to reach higher, and become more than you think you are capable of, to be courageous and stretch your limits.

Support is a very pleasant card to see in a reading, as it shows that the consultant benefits from positive influences. Either he will be able to reach his highest potential, or others will be there to help him achieve his goals.

As an asset

Your projects are up to a good start as they stand on solid ground, on good foundations. This might be due to your leadership and determination, allowing you to take control of the situation you are in. Or another possibility is that you are able to be supported by people around you.

As a problem

Support in this position is quite worrisome, as it can show that you lack leadership and determination, two qualities necessary to reach your objectives. The card can also show that no one around you offers their support and you are left alone to deal with your problems.

Additionally, it can also indicate that your projects don't have a firm base on which to stand, putting them in danger.

As advice

Support advises you to make alliances with others and get their help. You can achieve this by communicating effectively with others and trusting people surrounding you, or more specifically by surrounding yourself with people you can count on and having the skills necessary to advance your projects. Even if you feel that your projects stand on solid ground, it does not hurt to get advice.

As evolution

Support predicts a good progress for your projects, probably due to the help you can find around you. You were already up to a good start, standing on something firm, that you are able to solidify even more.

As outcome

Your projects have acquired a strong foundation and stability, certainly in part due to the help and protection of others. Be it real physical help, or advice, you were able to consolidate your goals up to the point where they can stand solid and provide you with a pleasant result.

40 - Beauty

(Beauté)

*"The quality of being pleasing and attractive, specially to look at.
The business of making people look attractive, using make-up, treatments, etc.
Something that is an excellent example of its type."*

Keywords: aesthetics, flourish, harmony, luxury, sensitivity, arts.

    A crowned heart is positioned above a flower.
    The language of flowers has been recognized for a long time, capable of stirring in us many feelings. For example a single red rose can make us immediately think of love, while a bouquet of flowers can remind us of invitations, dates, and many happy occasions. We give flowers to others when we want to express joy or contentment. The blooming flower we find on the card shows an expression of beauty and joy.
    The heart has been forever a symbol of love and compassion. Often seen as the center of our emotions, the

heart is synonymous with affections. On the card, the heart is crowned, giving to these emotions and feelings, a pure and profound sentiment.

Beauty evokes in us feelings of joy and sensuousness. All the elements present on the card seem to emphasize harmony, pleasure, and serenity. It could express not only a romantic bond, but also all kinds of emotional attachments we have. It can represent what awakens in us feelings of perfection or something aesthetically perfect.

Finally, the card can also represent everything that has to do with what we consider beautiful to observe, especially in the arts such as painting and sculpting. Think for instance of the Mona Lisa or Venus de Milo, the first words that come to mind are perfection, harmony and beauty.

As an asset

You display qualities such as harmony and sensitivity, that allow you to find the bright side in what you are dealing with. Your charisma and availability for others becomes an asset in the development of your plans.

As a problem

Your projects are suffering because you are lacking some essential qualities such as harmony, balance, or elegance in the solutions you're trying to find. There is an atmosphere around you where beauty and elegance cannot express themselves, like for instance looking at the bad side of things you are involved with.

As advice

Beauty suggests you to make the most of your qualities such as charm, attractiveness, and to emphasize around you how harmonious the situation is, in order to gain support for your projects. Ideally, you should look at the bright side and stay optimistic.

As evolution

Beauty shows that everything evolves harmoniously, allowing your projects to move in a very pleasant and balanced direction. There is a sense of accomplishment and well-being such that harmony prevails, leaving you with pleasant feelings.

As outcome

Beauty is forecasting serenity, balance and harmony, as it shows success in your projects. Effectively, pleasant solutions are found, giving you feelings of joy and pleasure.

41 - Heritage

(Héritage)

*"Property that is or may be inherited; an inheritance.
Features belonging to the culture of a particular society, such as traditions, language, or buildings, that were created in the past and still have historical importance.
A person's racial, ethnic, religious, or cultural background."*

Keywords: transmission, acquired wisdom, experience, relating to the past, succession, inheritance.

A green hourglass, a parchment, and a skull are laid on a flat surface.

The hourglass is symbolic of the inevitable passing of time, and as a result can be seen as a symbol of death, when we end our time on Earth, but also as a symbol of new beginnings or rebirth when we turn it over.

The skull symbolizes also life and in some cultures, is used in celebration for the deceased. Same as the hourglass, it has been associated with death and rebirth for a long time.

In the context of what these two symbols are dealing

with, the parchment in the middle of the card can be seen as a last will and testament, a written piece of paper where we enumerate our possessions and what should become of them once we leave this world.

As a result, the card can signify all things related to inheritance, what was left to us in the physical world. Literally, this card can be taken to the letter.

But symbolically we have to go beyond these mundane considerations, as esoterically death has always been considered more like transformation and renewal. In this context, Heritage becomes all the things that were or are transmitted to us, and they can go well beyond the material world.

In a wider context, Heritage represents the reception of past achievements or other things from the past that play an important role in the life of the consultant. Think about wisdom, knowledge, and all the experiences we acquired through our own actions or given to us by others, alive or not. An important aspect in this regard, is the non-materialistic things we received from our parents and ancestors.

As an asset

You are capable of making the most of the knowledge and experiences you acquired in the past, as this gave you the wisdom and mental capabilities to deal with what you are facing. All that experience can play a key role in trying to achieve your goals and obtain some gain.

As a problem

Two different types of problems can be seen with this card.

Either we lack the experience and knowledge needed, to

the point where it hurts our chances to achieve our objectives.

Or our past actions weight heavily on our situation. What we did in the past does not play in our favor.

As advice

You must rely on the experience you gained in the past, as it can constitute a considerable source of knowledge, both in intellectual and practical situations. It would be ill-advised to rush or act too drastically, as it would be better for you to reflect on what is happening and take the time to make plans based on your understanding of the situation. Just look into your past and remember how similar situations were dealt with.

As evolution

As long as what you're working on relies on past experiences and what worked favorably for you, everything should flow smoothly toward completion. After all, you gained a lot of knowledge in your life, and this is the right time to put it to work.

As outcome

Heritage, taken together with the influence of the planet Jupiter, promises favorable developments built on top of what is already there. This is due to your knowledge of the situation and the history of what already happened, or having already lived similar events. You can apply that learned experience to consolidate what is happening.

42 - Wisdom

(Sagesse)

*"The ability to use your knowledge and experience to make good decisions and judgements.
The body of knowledge and principles that develops within a specified society or period."*

Keywords: intelligence, maturity, serenity, mastery, life experience.

A crowned owl is watching us. The owl was the bird sacred to Athene, the goddess of wisdom, and shares the goddess's attributes. Owls are nocturnal, which makes them related to the Moon. This is just the opposite to the eagle, which can gaze directly at the Sun. Owls symbolize wisdom, intelligence, knowledge and clairvoyance. With its ability to unmask deception, the owl guides people who need to see the obvious, it invites you to see clearly in the dark. It can represent rational as well intuitive knowledge.

The owl has also been the traditional attribute of the seers, symbolizing their gift of second sight, exercised by their interpretation of omens.

The crown is an ornament worn on the head, symbolizing power and authority. Being present on top of the owl, it gives legitimacy to its wisdom and knowledge. The owl becomes an authority in the domains it rules.

Putting all these elements together, Wisdom represents the mind in a state of spiritual awakening, one where we can become aware that our mind has the capability to solve particular problems. As a result, the card can express all the qualities of the mind such as intelligence and knowledge.

Another important aspect is the knowledge we acquired through life, all the experiences and particular situation we lived, as that gives us valuable experience we can trust.

As an asset

You have the perspective and wisdom necessary to understand completely the situation you find yourself in. As a result, you are capable of using your experience and knowledge to solve any issue related to your problems, allowing you to move easily toward your goals.

As a problem

We can see two different aspects when Wisdom appears as problem. First, you might lack some of the knowledge needed for you to see your situation with all the necessary elements, or to have enough experience to make a wise decision.

The other possibility is that you think that you have enough knowledge and intellectual capabilities to solve your problems when it is clearly not the case.

As advice

Take the time to slow down and reflect on the situation

you're facing. This will allow you to apply past experience and your knowledge to what is happening. Using your maturity and common sense will allow you to direct what is happening in your life in the right direction.

As evolution

As Wisdom is first and foremost about what is going on on a mental plane, you are going to gain some valuable experience and maturity about what is goin on. Your capability to step back and wait, to understand better the situation you are facing and how it is evolving, allows you to use your wisdom in what is happening.

As outcome

As the card is under the influence of Jupiter, your project is more than probably successful as the planet represents among other things expansion and knowledge. But the kind of success we are talking about is more spiritual or about the knowledge gained rather than anything else. Wisdom allows you to accrue before all a sense of maturity and mastery.

43 - Fame

(La Renommée)

*"The state of being known or recognized by many people because of your achievements, skills, etc.
Widespread reputation, especially of a favorable character."*

Keywords: popularity, notoriety, celebrity, reputation, recognition.

The image shows a flag, a laurel wreath, and a trumpet, three objects often associated with fame and recognition.

Originally, flags were a visual icon for troops to rally around in fields of battle, as well as to avoid friendly fire incidents. But today, flags are more of a symbolic nature, representing a unifying force, such as the citizens of a country, or the members of an organization. They can be seen as a symbol of recognition for what they represent.

The symbolism of the laurel wreath comes from Greek mythology. It was later adopted by the Romans as symbols of military victory. In modern times, a laurel wreath is associated to many kinds of victories or success. It is no wonder that we find a laurel wreath drawn on many diplomas, a sure sign to be recognized for our expertise in some domain.

The trumpet was used to alert a crowd that some announcement or warning was about to take place. We can associate these customs to fame as it allowed people to congregate together for something of importance.

All three symbols taken together show the importance of something or someone. It is no wonder then that the Mage Edmond selected these to represent the situations when someone is recognized for what they did, or when the reputation of someone is such that they attract attention and notoriety. As such, the card can also represent popular people, the ones who reach a celebrity status for instance.

As an asset

Your popularity makes you attractive to others, other people involved in your situation appreciate you as a public figure, one that gives you some form of social recognition. The reputation you have acquired showcases your talent, experience, and skills to deal with what is happening.

As a problem

You lack support form others, and that hinders the possibility to reach your objectives. It might be because of your lack of fame, or because your reputation has been damaged. Whatever the reason, this inability to gain support or approbation from others will hurt your image.

As advice

Your notoriety is certainly the first asset you should exploit in order to reach your goals. To do that, you are advised to connect with others, and to try to increase your popularity. Your reputation is playing in your favor so try to get as much support as possible from others.

As evolution

Your projects should evolve in a very satisfying way, allowing you to increase your contacts and connections with others, impacting directly how you are perceived in a favorable way. The kind of evolution you can expect will be foremost about how you increase your notoriety, even if reaching your goals takes a very fortunate direction.

As outcome

First, Fame indicates positive repercussions on a personal level. Associated with the influence of Jupiter, you can expect an expansion of how people perceive you, boosting your popularity and recognition. All this bodes well for a successful outcome of your projects, especially in questions involving dealings with others.

44 - Hazard

(Le Hazard)

*"The effect of unpredictable and unanalyzable forces in determining events.
A chance event.
To offer or present at a risk."*

Keywords: unforeseen events, opportunities, movement, luck, dynamism.

A golden crown lays on top of a winged wheel.
The wheel has been one of the most important inventions for mankind. It effectively represented a major turning point in human civilization, as it gave the ability to work more efficiently and travel move quickly. Since then, wheels have played an important role both in transport and industry.
If we add the wings, they gives us not only the ability to fly, but also the notion of improvement in what we are doing, giving us freedom and creativity.
The crown is an ornament representing authority, and as

such gives us the means to control what is happening, giving to that wheel a notion of controlled direction, of us leading what is happening in the direction we want. As a result, the wheel is not really a free movement, but one we control.

Putting all these together, Hazard represents first and foremost movement, sometimes unpredictable, but that allows a situation to evolve. It will appear in situations where we want things to move, and even if we try to control in which direction it will evolve, there is always an element of unpredictability associated with it.

Of course, Hazard can also represent the chances we are taking in life, unforeseen events, strokes of luck or twists of fate. Whatever it is, it will always represent a dynamic situation, evolving, never something static.

Last, the wheel shown in this card can make us think about transportation, and Hazard can represent bikes, cars, etc. even aircrafts as there is a pair of wings drawn on the card.

As an asset

Chance is on your side, a lucky event allows you to get closer to your goals and aspirations. Your dynamism allows you to take control of what is going on and you have the energy to make the most of it. You are not afraid of changes, and take advantage of them.

As a problem

Hazard will often represent a situation where nothing is happening, or more exactly where any movement forward has been stopped or blocked, and opportunities of development are not available to you. There might be several reasons why this is happening. Maybe chance is not on your side and you are too pessimistic to make things evolve in your favor. Or there is a complete lack of will or energy from your part, leaving you in a stale situation. Your projects might also evolve in a direction you were not expecting, resulting in delays or setbacks.

As advice

With Hazard, you are highly advised to follow your lucky star and take some action, to do what is necessary to make your situation evolve. There is of course a risk involved as the card always shows a notion of unforeseen events happening, but taking chances should be beneficial for your projects. Of course, this can result in being forced to slightly change direction, going through trials and errors in moving forward.

As evolution

Opportunities will come your way. The evolution of your projects will not go in a straight line, expect developments and a progression to happen, but some events might be more the result of chance or external events rather than your own actions. Whatever the situation, you will certainly see it evolve.

As outcome

Together with the expansion represented by the influence of Jupiter, you can expect growth and expansion for your projects, luck is more than probably on your side. If you are asking about a situation that was stuck, Hazard is certainly one of the best cards to get.

45 - Happiness

(Bonheur)

*"The feeling of being pleased or happy.
A state of well-being and contentment."*

Keywords: joy, success, pleasure, conviviality, wealth.

    A hand outstretched from a cloud is receiving a red star and a golden crown. The hand is open, palm up, in a gesture of receiving something. That position of the palm represents us receiving what is on top of it, the star and the crown.

    The Mage Edmond selected two important objects given to us. The star has always been a symbol of hope. Old navigators, for instance, used them to look for the direction in which they had to sail to reach their destination. Stars have become symbols of positivity, and guidance. We usually associated them with good luck, wishes, good omens. For instance, we make a wish when seeing a shooting star.

    Crowns are a symbol of royalty. They give to their bearer power and authority, the possibility to command others.

Putting everything together, that open hand is receiving a symbol of spiritual guidance and another one of power. If we add the influence of Jupiter, the one receiving this card is given quite important attributes, both on a spiritual and material level.

Happiness shows a complete state of happiness and fullness, and as such represents joy and well-being. Happiness is certainly one of the most rewarding cards in the oracle.

As an asset

You are in a very good place to attack your problems and try to reach your goals. The way you express feelings of joy and your charisma will make people react positively to your attitude, motivating them to give you a hand in whatever you are doing.

As a problem

Happiness shows a joyless attitude and a total lack of happiness. Being such a favorable card, when it is seen as a problem, it can forecast a very difficult situation, proportionally as bad as it was good as an asset. Success is not coming for the querent, it shows that events are taking a bad turn, it could even lead you to a very depressed state.

As advice

Be happy and good things will come to you. This is maybe a little bit exaggerated, but this is the gist of the attitude to have when Happiness comes as advice. Put yourself in a positive and optimistic state of mind, and as a consequence your uplifting attitude will allow you to see problems with a more optimistic view and to find satisfying solutions more easily.

As evolution

Your projects are evolving the way you would like to, and that gives you a lot of pleasure. In that sense, it is not really about finding a solution to every little detail, but rather in seeing your situation evolving in a direction that gives you first and foremost a satisfying outlook on what is happening.

As outcome

Happiness is certainly a good omen that you have reached your objectives. At a minimum, you find yourself surrounded with joy and pleasure, certainly a sign that you have reached a situation giving you satisfaction. Even if the success was not complete, the outcome is still very satisfying.

Saturn

Saturn is the sixth planet from the Sun, and the second largest of the Solar system, after Jupiter. It is certainly the most recognizable, with its rings, and it can be seen from Earth with the help of a telescope.

Saturn was named after the Roman god of agriculture. According to myth, Saturn introduced agriculture to his people by teaching them how to farm the land. Saturn was also the Roman god of time, probably because it was the slowest of the planets visible in the Solar system.

In Roman mythology, Saturn was the father of Jupiter. Saturn was also identified with the Greek god Cronus. Exiled form Olympus by Zeus, he ruled Latium, an ancient region of Italy.

In astrology, Saturn reflects wisdom, discipline, and

karma. It shines a light in areas of your life where you need to grow. Similar to the planet's slow moving pace, Saturn is about the long haul, persistence, and patience: it is more about milestones and long term goals.

Symbolically, Saturn represents time and matter. It is the limitation of defined things, bringing concepts to reality, spirit to body, thoughts to words, life to death.

Saturn represents the restrictive principle, the difficulties, blocks, what is laborious and takes time in a person's life. Saturn is often represented as an old man, giving the planet notions of solitude, isolation, misfortune, time passing and karma. It shows what diminishes and fades in our lives.

All these aspects are well represented on the seven Saturnian cards. We can see misfortune in Misfortune (46), what diminishes and fades in Sterility (46), the unfortunate consequences of the passage of time in Fatality (48), Grace (49) is the only card in this series giving hope by divine intervention, slow destruction in Ruin (50), time passing in Delay (51), and solitude in Cloister (52).

46 - Misfortune

(Infortune)

"An event or conjunction of events that causes an unfortunate or distressing result: bad luck.
An unhappy situation.
A distressing or unfortunate incident or event."

Keywords: difficulties, handicap, bad luck, unfortunate events, problematic situation.

An old woman dressed in rags is moving painfully with the help of a crutch. She is barefoot, wearing a kerchief, an old bag under her arm, all signs showing how poor she is. The prominent chin, hooked nose, recessed mouth, and severe look give the stereotypical image of an old hag.

Under the influence of Saturn, we can easily imagine how unfortunate she looks. This impression is further defined by her posture, bent, she seems to move with difficulty, and the stance of her right hand, palm up, reminds us of beggars.

Misfortune warns us of unfortunate events happening in

our life, all the hazards and bad turns it can take. There is so much austerity shown in this card, she went through a lot and is trying to survive. However she is still begging and moving forward, she does not give up, she continues to try to survive in her arduous environment.

The card also highlights the dangers of not being surrounded by others, the problems related to solitude, old age, and lack of resources.

As an asset

When a situation becomes as bad as described by Misfortune, there isn't really any favorable aspect to look for. The only positive point you could see is to continue trying to achieve your goals, against all odds, the courage you show facing adversity is remarkable.

As a problem

You are facing difficulties to move toward your goals. These can manifest themselves as bad luck, twists of fate, or you might be facing a situation which is almost impossible to solve. It can be up to the point where you will be demoralized and left with a feeling of not being able to do anything about it.

As advice

The most important sign on this card is that the woman continues to move forward, and this particular point is showing what we should do. So, even if the circumstances around our issues are far from perfect, we must continue to try to reach our objectives. In order to do this, we must try to control our resources and not waste them on superficial aspects of our projects. Try to mobilize what is in your control to go to the essential.

As evolution

Your projects are not evolving in a satisfying way, there is a huge feeling of being unsatisfied and restricted by their progression. You're looking more into a lot of energy wasted, resulting in difficulties to move forward. Even if some very small progress is achieved, it is not going to be significant, as your are facing bad luck and some twists of fate are not playing at all in your favor.

As outcome

Misfortune evokes a complete lack of luck in what you're trying to achieve, and a lot of difficulties to get there. This card is not really telling you that you cannot reach your goals, but if you do, it will cost you a lot of energy and you will feel miserable in the position you will find yourself in. Think for instance of someone staying in a relationship or a job where you feel completely overwhelmed and despondent.

47 - Sterility

(Stérilité)

*"Failing to bear or incapable of producing fruit or spores.
Failing to produce or incapable of producing offspring.
Incapable of germinating.
Lacking in stimulating or intellectual quality."*

Keywords: barren, unproductive, infertile, incapacity, stalemate.

In the middle of a turbulent sea, rocks forming small mountains are emerging from the water. These peaks are quite steep, and completely barren.

Sterility reminds us a lot of Departure (12). We find the same kind of rocks, barren of all vegetation or life. The difference being that on this card, we don't see any bird, there is nothing giving us the capability of escaping from the island.

As there is nothing growing, no vegetation and no life, the main signification for this card is one of abandonment and deprivation, finding oneself in a place or situation where nothing grows, giving us a feeling of exclusion and abandonment.

We could also additionally see this cards as a period in our life when we are not interested by materialism. As everything is barren, it is the perfect place to reflect on our problems without any distraction. The perfect place to meditate and think about the situation we are in.

As an asset

As you are facing limitations and restrictions, to the point where no physical or emotional action is possible in order to move your objectives forward, you are left with only the possibility to reflect on what is going on around you, delaying your plans for later.

As a problem

You are facing a difficult situation, one in which every effort you make is not bringing much result. Whatever you try, your efforts do not bring fruit, no tangible result is reached. The only think you are left with is your mind, to try to find a solution for later, when you might be able to get out of the unfavorable place you find yourself in.

As advice

As the situation you are in does not provide anything useful in order to reach your goals, you should start restricting yourself to doing the minimum and let the situation evolve by itself. Just limit the resources available to you, whatever they are, time, money or something else.

As evolution

Sterility, together with the energy of Saturn, evokes feelings of constriction and restriction. Nothing new is coming, the situation you are in does not bear any fruitful development and does not change. There is a sense of a climate where your projects cannot grow at all, they can only decline due to the barren environment you are facing.

As outcome

Sterility does not show any satisfaction or success in the situation you are facing. On the contrary, everything seems to restrict, giving a feeling of austerity and decline. It could be a job leading to a place that does not give you any joy or advancement, or a sentimental environment where you feel neglected.

48 - Fatality

(Fatalité)

"The quality or state of causing death or destruction. The quality or condition of being destined for disaster. Something established by fate."

Keywords: deadline, test of time, destiny, fate, transformation.

    A man is facing us, holding a scythe with his right hand, and a whip with the left.
    The scythe is an object that was used in agriculture, and is still in used today in some less developed regions, for the harvest, and to cut weeds of all sorts. The main usage is the harvest, which is done at the end of summer or early fall, when crops are ready to be reaped. As such, the harvest can represent something ending, but more importantly the reaping of what is ready. And this cycle repeats itself yearly, showing symbolically cycles of death and rebirth.
    The whip expresses an idea of punishment, and the power to dominate. But it can also be used in rituals of

flagellation.

Taken together, these two objects that the man is holding give him power of domination and the capability to cut. If we link this with the influence of Saturn, and the inevitability of fate found in the word fatality, we can get the feeling of a card expressing things that are outside of our control, things that finds us powerless facing something bigger than us.

Fatality makes us think of our destiny and how powerless we can be facing it. The scythe cuts, the grim reaper comes for all of us. Without being negative to the extreme and thinking about death, Fatality can express all the things that happen in our lives over which we have no control and often feel that they restrict us in some way. Fatality tells us that we have no freedom to act in some cases.

As an asset

As the whip corrects and the scythe cuts, you are able to symbolically use these tools to your advantage. You can easily correct what needs to be corrected, cut what does not serve you anymore, and adapt to new cycles, when your objectives take another direction.

As a problem

Fatality shows difficulties to adapt to changes and transformations. You might struggle to react facing these changes, or simply be reticent, putting you in a situation that could leave you blocked and not able to pursue your goals.

As advice

Fatality suggests that you should brainstorm on what you want to achieve, and think deeply about it and its consequences. You should consider what needs to be blocked or cut, what actions need to be done to correct what is happening in order to move forward in the right direction. You might also need to reconsider the validity of what you want, as you might want to change direction or even not move further toward the goals you defined earlier.

As evolution

Before anything else, Fatality is about cycles, some inevitable endings. As a result, you might expect your projects to change direction, develop differently, or be cut. Your adaptation to changes is going to be very important in order to maintain focus on your goal.

As outcome

The card shows the end of a cycle, something is terminated. As such, in addition to the restrictive notion of Saturn, it is difficult to see any success when Fatality expresses an outcome. For instance, expect your current job to be terminated or deeply transformed, or your relationship to end.

49 - Grace

(La Grâce)

"A unmerited divine assistance given to humans for their regeneration or sanctification.
Approval, favor.
A charming or attractive trait or characteristic."

Keywords: blessing, generosity, spiritual protection, favor, absolution.

    A dove, wings deployed, is descending from the sky toward the earth. The dove flies in a triangle of light.
    Doves have always been symbols of peace, spirituality, and hope. The dove has also been associated with the Bible, which seems important here because of the triangle surrounding it. In the Old Testament, a dove is a symbol of reconciliation, forgiveness, and peace. In the book of Genesis, after the flood, a dove returned to Noah holding an olive leaf. They also often appear on banners and signs at events promoting peace.
    The triangle of light represents the trinity, making

reference to the divine and the sacred.

Among all the cards under the influence of Saturn, with most of them depicting difficult situations or events, Grace brings a note of hope with its light and spiritual aspect.

In this card, with the dove flying from the sky towards the earth, Grace is bringing the divine to more mundane things, giving us a sense of unity, of something harmonious.

Grace indicates that a "divine" intervention is always possible, regardless of the situation we find ourselves in, that we are able to receive a favor, and as such, it brings us some form of divine inspiration.

As an asset

Grace highlights your spiritual qualities. As we are still under the influence of Saturn, among all the restrictions and setbacks in your projects, you retain a sense of hope and optimism that allows you to persevere in the direction you chose.

As a problem

You will find yourself facing difficulties in obtaining favors or help from others around you, making it difficult for you to improve your chances of moving forward with your projects. As you are not getting any support, you can expect delays and obstacles in the way your projects will progress.

As advice

Grace is first and foremost about hope. Practically, this means that you should have faith in your projects, even if they don't seem to move forward or if they seem to take a turn for the worse. Grace tells you to continue against all odds. You will, at a minimum, obtain a meaningful experience with your enterprise; Grace will more than probably allow you to transform your projects and move them in the right direction.

As evolution

Grace acts as a protection, as it tells you first to always keep hope. So, even if your projects seem to take an unsatisfactory direction, there are still feelings of protection and blessings prevailing. There is always hope, light at the end of the tunnel, maybe in a context of pain and difficulties, but with some effort something will still come at the end.

As outcome

Grace shows a happy conclusion to the situation you are in, which can be considered successful, because of some external help or support you got. With Grace, there is always something that seems providential in what happened, and that allows you to solve your problems or fix your situation. Among all the unfavorable Saturn cards, Grace is the one giving you a beacon of hope.

50 - Ruin

(Ruine)

*"To spoil or destroy something completely.
To cause a person or company to lose all their money, or their good reputation.
The broken parts that are left of a building or town that has been destroyed by bombs, fire, etc."*

Keywords: old, old fashioned, outdated, collapse, destruction, debacle.

A tower is collapsing, the top is separated from the base, many stones are falling down. Visually, this card reminds us of Accident (38), where there is also a tower with the top falling down. The main difference between the two cards, is that in Ruin, we lose the sudden event represented by lightning. In Ruin, the top collapses due to the effects of time. Ruin can also remind us of Penates (16), and what can happen when we don't act and let time degrade what was once great.

Symbolically, towers represent an image of wealth,

success, strength and power. But all these qualities have been tested by the Saturnian influences of restriction and mostly time passing. And with time passing, the construction has become less sturdy, to the point where it starts to degrade sufficiently to begin to lose its structure. What remains are only vestiges of a glorious past.

Ruin can show buildings and constructions that have collapsed, or are at least partially destroyed. But if we take a more symbolic point of view, Ruin is not a good omen for our projects, as it shows the relentless passage of time that can result in something that was once sturdy becoming fragile or destroyed. Think of a great job that has become obsolete, or a once happy marriage where only difficulties remain.

In general, Ruin will show a situation that deteriorates over time.

As an asset

Per its nature, it becomes very difficult to find any asset in Ruin, except maybe to let go and not put any more resources into something that does not serve you anymore, letting it degenerate over time. But more often, you will face a situation where you do not get much help. The only thing you can do, is count on yourself, and look at your past experience. Look especially at what caused problems and what ended up in failure, that can indicate what you need to improve going forward.

As a problem

You find yourself in a very difficult situation due to past problems. These might be, for instance, earlier problems in a relationship that reverberates in the present, bad past decisions in your job, or past debts not yet paid. Whatever it is, you are dragging a difficult past in the present.

As advice

There is not much you can do. Take a little bit the same attitude than the one you would have in Sterility (47), just limit your efforts to a strict minimum, wait, there might be a better time later. As the situation is already badly damaged, it is better to do nothing in order to avoid more problems. The problem is that if you want to persevere, you will have to constantly try to repair some aspects, but there is not much hope to get back to something sturdy.

As evolution

Ruin will show a slow disintegration of the situation you find yourself in. Whatever the state of your project or situation is when asking your question, you can expect a slow degradation. If we take the image of a tower, where the top will collapse first, your situation will follow the same direction, with superficial things falling down first, then more substantial ones.

As outcome

Ruin does not bode well at all for your projects, as it shows the effect of time disintegrating everything with its passage. At most, all you can expect is maybe in some cases for some foundations to remain, but not much else.

51 - Delay

(Retard)

*"To make something happen at a later time than originally planned or expected.
To cause someone or something to be slow or late.
To not act quickly or immediately."*

Keywords: slowness, waiting, setback, slowdown, unforeseen event,

    A wheel is stuck between two cliffs. The wheel reminds us of Hazard (44), except that it lost its wings and there is no crown. All the artifacts capable of helping that wheel move or allowing us to take a decision have been removed. All these elements correspond well to the associated planets, as the expansion of Jupiter has been replaced by the restrictions of Saturn.
    In Delay, the atmosphere is static, the wheel is immobile, incapable of moving without giving it a humongous effort or counting on an external intervention.
    As we saw earlier, wheels are important because they

allow movement, they allow something to move quickly. As such, with the wheel blocked, Delay shows situations where we encounter obstacles that slow us down significantly. This might be due to an unforeseen event, the querent's fault, or any circumstances outside of their control. The result is such that time will be necessary to try to unblock the situation and get things moving again, putting us in a position where we might not be able to reach our objectives.

As an asset

This might feel strange, but as an asset we have to look how we can implement the difficulties represented by Delay to our advantage. What works in our favor the most, is that we are capable of slowing down or blocking the situation we are involved in. Delaying the evolution of something will allow us to have the time to evaluate it better and eventually prepare countermeasures, or simply to get out of something too difficult to manage.

As a problem

Delay evokes the slowness happening around a situation and how it can become problematic. You will have to deal with the consequences of needing more time than planned or discussed to reach your objectives. You are faced with events that must develop quickly, but facing setback after setback, putting in jeopardy the final outcome.

As advice

Take your time, slow down the pace of what is happening. Patience is king, it would be better for your own sake to remove any form of impulsivity from the equation, there are situations in which things are better developed when the progression is slow.

As evolution

Not much is happening, everything slows down, or even stops. You might be facing unforeseen obstacles or burdens difficult to solve. These might take a lot of time and require a lot of energy to solve them.

As outcome

Delay shows very well the restrictive aspects of Saturn, as well as time passing, as it is forecasting delays, a slowness that could even lead to nothing happening at all for a long time. It is difficult in these conditions to forecast what will be the long term consequences of the delays occurred, but they do not bode well for a favorable outcome. On the contrary, you might expect to find yourself in a situation which is not resolved, one that will require more effort to achieve any kind of result.

52 - Cloister

(Cloitre)

*"A monastic establishment.
An area within a monastery or convent to which the religious are normally restricted.
A covered passage on the side of a court usually having one side walled and the other an open arcade or colonnade."*

Keywords: isolation, loneliness, renunciation, monastery, grid, fence.

 A narrow entrance is barred with a portcullis. A portcullis is a vertically closing gate that was typically found in medieval castles and fortifications. It was made of a lattice grille, often in metal. By itself, this element is already telling us of a location which is closed to most people. It can be seen, depending on which side we stand, as a protection for the people enclosed, or as a gate not allowing intrusion.

 As we can see, its main function is to have a separation allowing a relatively small group of people to be separated from a larger one. And the word "cloister" gives us something similar, as it tells us of a secluded place, such as a monastery, where people can pray or meditate.

Putting all this together, Cloister shows us a place where we can withdraw from the world and shelter in an place suited to reflection and meditation. A place where we can isolate ourselves from our everyday environment, finding quietness and an excellent atmosphere for contemplation.

There is another aspect of Cloister which can be less auspicious. If we add the energies of Saturn, basically restriction and time passing, it can mean that we find ourselves placed in an environment where we close ourselves off to others, isolated and probably so lonely that it becomes problematic.

A cloister is `another name for a monastery; it could represent places of worship, or even historical places and monuments.

As an asset

One of your great qualities is that you are capable of moving yourself out of the hubbub surrounding your problems. That allows you to take the necessary time to isolate yourself and reflect on what is going on.

As a problem

Isolation and an attitude of being closed up are working against you. Your situation might require to communicate with others and to open what is going on to more people, but your attitude is just the opposite, you are symbolically closing the portcullis instead of opening it, hurting your chances of success.

As advice

Similar to card Delay (49), the best advice would be to

take time to meditate and reflect alone on what is happening. Even going further, going on a retreat or a place outside of all the noise of everyday life would be beneficial to the well-being of your projects. The main difference with Delay, is that in Cloister, there is no obstacle to consider, the retreat from normal life is voluntary.

As evolution

Cloister does not really show an active evolution, but rather a direction towards isolation and even pause. The card expresses more a time when we isolate ourselves to reflect on the situation and how to make it evolve rather than acting.

As outcome

If the intended outcome of what you are involved with evokes some kind of isolation or restrictions from regular life, Cloister would be a success. For every other case, Cloister is too restrictive to show a situation coming to fruition. It is more about cases where we close ourselves to others.

Part 3
Reading the Cards

*Spreads are the grammar we need to
link everything together*

Introduction

In regards to the techniques that we can use, reading the oracle Belline is not much different than reading the tarot. Of course the cards don't look the same and their meanings are quite different, but that does not mean that we should use a totally different approach when reading them. We can certainly use the same strategies when it comes to asking a question or what kind of spread to use.

If you look around, there are hundreds of spreads available, some specialized in different subjects, for example about love, work, or something else. There are even complete books dedicated to spreads and how to construct one.

This is certainly an interesting approach that you can use with these cards. At the end of this section, I will explain a similar technique on how to respond to a question with one card. But in my opinion, it is much better to know just a few spreads, and to know them well. It is also my experience that always using the same spreads will increase your confidence in them.

A good spread should be versatile and flexible enough to be useful in many different situations and domains. By using the same spread over and over, you will develop a special bond with it, and know the shortcuts that will make it more efficient when you read it.

You will find in this section the three spreads I use the most: the Advice, the French Cross, and the Snapshot. The Advice is used to look at how someone should behave facing a problem. The French Cross allows you to analyze any situation in detail. The Snapshot is used for a general reading and to determine quickly what aspects of the querent's life cause problems, which then can be examined with one of the other spreads. One question, one card, will show you how to quickly respond efficiently to a simple upright.

Used together in a session, they will allow you to respond to any question someone could ask during a consultation. Over the years, I have tested these spreads thousands of times, and always found them extremely reliable. Over time, they became the cornerstone of my divination practice.

For each spread, two examples on how to use them will be given.

But even before talking spreads and doing readings, let's start this section with some very important aspects: how to ask a good question, and how to shuffle and lay down the cards. I will also give my opinion on reversed cards and why I don't use them with the oracle Belline.

There is one aspect I don't want to deal with in this book, rituals. How you store your cards, how to clean them, listening to music during a reading, etc. are left to each reader and their own belief. I will just say that whatever you do, is a valid way of doing it. There is no right or wrong way, as long as you do as you believe you should do.

The Question

One of the most important and often overlooked elements in a reading is the question. It seems obvious, but there would be no reading session or divination if there was no question asked. As I heard several times, if you want better answers, ask better questions.

A good question should be open ended, to the point, and clear in its intent, in order to provide a meaningful response. In order to achieve this, you need to establish a good dialog with the querent, be curious and have a good discussion about what your querent really wants to know. In order to proceed, you need at least a general idea of what your session should be about. Knowing how to ask good question is essential to provide the best possible service to your clients.

The task is not always easy, but a few simple principles can help you.

Use positive terms.

Always try to avoid negative questions. Instead, try to always rephrase your questions in a positive way.

For instance, do not ask if your partner is leaving, but rather how your relationship with your partner will evolve. Or do not ask if you are going to be laid off. Instead, you might want to ask how your job with your current company will evolve. That will tell you, not only if you will stay or leave, but also the circumstances surrounding your situation.

The problem with negative questions has to do with how we associate favorable or unfavorable cards. If we consider the question as "a project" that you ask your oracle about, does a favorable card announce the success of your endeavor, or the success of the project you are asking about?

For instance, if you ask if you will lose your job, does the card Success (5) announces that you keep your job, or that the project of losing it will succeed? Same idea with leaving your partner. Does the same Success card announces a reconciliation of the couple, or the success of leaving your partner?

Negative questions lead to ambiguous answers. Try to always ask your question in a positive, more constructive way.

Ask an open question instead of a yes/no question.

A yes/no question will tell you if something will happen or not, nothing more. This means that you have to use your cards in a different way than you usually do. In order to get a valid answer, you would have to associate each card with a positive or negative result, and use that as your answer.

This way of proceeding is not very useful as it does not give much information to your querent. You would not get more information than you would when using a pendulum or tossing a coin. You would lose valuable information that your cards can give you.

If instead you are asking for the evolution of a situation, you will get much more information on what is happening in addition to be able to reply if yes or no what you are asking about is going to happen.

Ask for instance how will your interview will go, instead of if you will get the job, yes or no.

Use simple questions, with only one option.

It seems obvious that, when doing a spread, it should lead to a response for a single question. Multiple questions, or questions with multiple options, should be treated by doing a spread for each one.

For instance, do not ask if you're going to move to Miami or New York. Instead, ask the cards to show you what you need to know if you move to Miami. Then ask what you should know if you move New York. Eventually you could also ask what you should know if you move somewhere else, and as another option what will happen if you don't move. Asking more questions, each one targeted to a simple option, will give you not only more meaningful information, but also a more complete view of your situation.

To take another example, do not ask if your ex is coming

back and then if you're going to be happy together. That's two different questions, with the second one completely depending on the first. It would be better to first ask how your situation is going to evolve with your ex. And if it seems that you will get back together, ask how your feelings for your ex will evolve.

Ask about someone, not something.
Objects are static, they don't do anything, while people do. In that way, it is always better to ask about someone rather than something.

Let's take the example of a relationship. It is of course interesting to ask how the relationship will evolve, as it can give a general idea of what is happening around the couple. But a relationship evolving in a positive way does not mean that the two partners are happy with each other.

There are many cases where one of the partners feels fulfilled while the other feels neglected. In such a case, it would be very beneficial for your querent to do more than one reading, first for the relationship itself as it will allow to get a general idea, then for each partner and how they will feel in the relationship.

Or let's say that you would like to sell a house. Whatever happens, the house will stay static and will do nothing. You are dealing with yourself as the seller, eventually a real estate agent, and potential buyers, who will probably need a mortgage and might have their own real estate agent. A lot of people who will each act in their own interest. A better session would be to start by asking what you should do in order to improve your chances to sell your house in your best interest. Then you could look into how to attract more buyers, etc.

Avoid vague or subjective terms.

You should remove vague and subjective terms from your questions, as they can have different meanings for different people. For instance, your querent might ask how soon he will get a new job, and "soon" might mean a few weeks for him while you're thinking in months. Or if the querent is asking how to get a job with a decent salary, what means "decent"? Different people will have different opinions on these terms.

You should define precise terms in your questions. For these examples, you could ask if the querent will get a new job in the next eight weeks, or any period of time you both agree on. Or replace the "decent" salary with "X dollars or more", putting a minimum amount that the querent has in mind.

Ask as many questions as necessary.

Responding to your querent's concerns is rarely possible if you try to use only one spread and respond to a single question. Most of the time, your querent will have a complex issue, and often it is much better to split his concerns into smaller questions, that will allow you to give a much better overall response.

As you will see, many relationship, job or other subjects, will lead to many sub-questions once the main issue has been treated. For instance, a relationship evolving into a separation might lead to a series of concerns, such as financial assets, moving somewhere else, children, etc.

Shuffling and Laying Out the Cards

There are many different ways to shuffle and lay out the cards. The three main known methods are:

- Riffle shuffle - this is a classic technique that is used in casinos and around bridge circles, because it is supposed to be a very good way to randomize a deck of cards. The basic principle is that you separate your deck into two stacks having about the same number of cards, and putting them close together, you bend the cards and allow them in intersect. If you have never heard about this method, there are many videos on the internet that can help you to learn it.
- Overhand shuffle - this is certainly the simplest way to shuffle a pack of cards in an efficient way. It is also very popular because, compared to the riffle shuffle, it is much simpler to execute for most people. This shuffle is performed by holding the deck face down in one hand, and then sliding some cards from the top of the deck to the other hand, repeating the operation until the whole deck is transferred.
- Mixing on the table - this is not a shuffle by itself, but a an easy way to randomize your cards. You simply put all your cards on the table and move them around with your two hands in a chaotic way. When done, you simply put them back together.

When starting with divination, it is normal to feel lost and not know which method to use. Like with any other rituals linked to divination, the best way to proceed is to try them all and then pick the one that you feel works the best for you. They are all valid, just decide at some point which method you prefer and stick to it. Creating habits and using always the same method will increase your confidence in the process.

The next step is what some people call cutting the deck. Some people even look at the cards generated during this process, looking at the card in the middle of the pack revealed when cutting, and the card at the bottom. For most, the two cards showed by the cut indicate the state of mind of the querent concerning their question. While many readers do it, I personally never found this process useful in my readings. I'd rather put what the cut can represent as positions in the spread that were decided in advance and start interpreting these.

There are also different methods used to draw the cards and lay them out into the predefined places of the spread. Same as when shuffling, they all work fine, and different readers use different techniques. The two main ones are to pick cards from the top of the deck, or to fan the cards on the table and randomly select them.

The way I do it after many years of practice, is to overhand shuffle, fan the deck and randomly pick the cards I need. The main reasons why I do overhand shuffling is that, even after all these years and thousands of shuffles, I never mastered correctly the art of riffle shuffling. Another reason is that the bending of the cards when doing a riffle shuffle can, with time, damage your cards.

On the subject of shuffling, there remains a last point, something which is often asked by beginners. Who should shuffle the cards, the querent or the reader?

Over time, I tried both ways, and both methods work fine. I have never seen a difference in the accuracy in my readings when using one method over the other. My way of doing it is to shuffle myself for two main reasons. First, I do a lot of readings over video and in that case, I am the only one physically present to shuffle. Second, most consultants, when they come to see you for a reading, are nervous about the process and find it difficult to mix the cards. Letting them shuffle can often result in cards bent or falling to the floor.

Introduction

Reversed Cards

A question I get a lot from students and that I also see young readers ask inevitably is: should we use reversed cards? By this, I mean cards that fall upside-down and are read that way during a reading. This is a legitimate question, which has split the world of divination for a very long time.

Personally, I do not use them in my practice. If by chance a card appears reversed, I simply turn it to have it upright. I would strongly advise you to act the same way and not use reversed cards, for many reasons that we are going to look at in detail.

- Many deck backs are not symmetrical. Even the pattern of stars on the original oracle Belline is not symmetrical. With a little bit of experience and a good eye, when spreading the cards, you will be able to see the ones which are upright, and the ones which are reversed. This, of course, defeats the argument that a reading should use completely randomized cards as you are able to select what pleases you at will.
- They double the number of of meanings, your 52 cards will have 104 meanings. This can be a tempting argument if you use only one card per question. But at the same time, the oracle Belline has about the same number of favorable and unfavorable cards, making it well balanced, even if you use only upright cards. I like simplicity, why would I complicate unnecessarily something that works.
- Most spreads have positions indicating a favorable or unfavorable aspect of a question. This complicates a lot the use of reversed cards, and this is probably the point with which most beginners, and not so beginning readers struggle. How do you interpret a bad card

reversed in an unfavorable positions, or how do you interpret a good reversed card in a favorable position? I never found a satisfying response to this argument.
- They don't add nuance. Spreads are not a succession of one card readings. When interpreting a spread, you must take into account all the cards, and how they interact with each other. When doing a five-cards reading with only upright cards, we already have 311,875,200 possible combinations. Nuance comes from looking how everything balances together.
- They don't make your readings flow. Looking at reversed cards and trying to understand what they mean will, without a shadow of a doubt, put you into thinking mode instead of keeping your intuition flowing. I always found that by constantly interrupting the flow of what we see by putting on our thinking hat does not allow for a smooth delivery of what is going on.
- They do not align with my philosophy. This point is just a personal opinion, but I would never look at a piece of art or a picture reversed. In fact, for everything we look at in life, we look at it in an upside position. I don't see anybody reading a reversed book, or taking a reversed stance when looking at something in the street or anywhere else. In that case, why would I make an exception for reading cards?

The Advice Spread

The Advice Spread is is a very simple one that will allow you to understand better what could be done moving forward when facing a particular situation.

Of course, it is always interesting to look at how a situation will evolve, or what will happen in the life of the querent. But, as a starting point, or after having looked at the evolution of what the querent is asking about, it would be interesting to know how to act. This probably goes back to the fact that I don't believe in fate, but in my opinion taking ownership of our responsibilities, and knowing how to act or not to act in a particular situation, is very important.

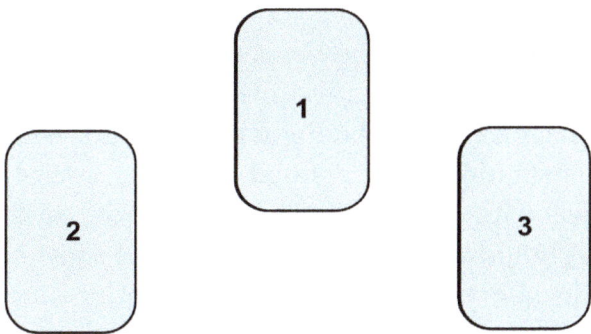

The Advice Spread is made of three cards.
- Position 1 represents the energies facing the querent and their situation. It will explain the attitude of the querent facing their situation, how they feel about it and how they behave, what kind of energies they spend trying to move forward.
- Position 2 represents what the querent should do facing their situation. It will explain what is the best course of action, how the querent should behave, what kind of energies they should deploy in order to reach their goal.

- Position 3 represents what the querent should not do moving forward. It will explain what is the worse course of action, how the querent should not behave, what kind of energies they should not deploy in order to reach their goal.

The principal aspect when interpreting this spread is to look together at positions (2) and (3) in the context of position (1). What is important is reading the two cards together, the contrast between them being often a significant factor. There is a fine line between what to do and what not to do, that the querent should adopt.

Of course, this spread is about advice, not what will happen to your situation. While the cards will express the best way for the querent to act and not act, this does not guarantee that the querent will get their wish fulfilled.

For example, a querent asking how to act in order to get a job or find a partner does not guarantee that it will happen. The cards should be understood as giving advice on how best to deal with a situation. The fact that the cards explain how you should act or not act indicate the most beneficial way for the querent to proceed forward, nothing more.

The case of Debbie

Debbie is responsible for managing a store and is having some problems with one of her salesmen. She is asking how she should act with him.

With Trial as the energies facing Debbie, we can see immediately that the environment between her and the salesman is not very productive. We're looking mostly at clashes, discussions, situations where they symbolically cross swords, and not leading to something quieter nor to any peaceful solution.

With Inconstancy, the advice is for Debbie to stay

flexible, staying set in her position would be problematic. She should look carefully at the situation and however it evolves, in order to be able to adapt her position quickly, she would benefit from having quick reactions to what is happening.

With Thought - Friendship in the position of what not to do, she should not have a laidback stance on how she treats the salesman, a friendly attitude is not going to be beneficial to her. After all, she is the manager and she should not show any hesitation to assert her authority, as their professional relation is not on an equal level.

Being quick-witted, showing who is the boss, are two important aspects indicating how she should act. She can expect more confrontations, even having to let the matter go to a higher authority, or human resources.

Is Bob going to get what he is asking for?

Bob is looking at selling his home and has one offer that he estimates too low. How should he deal with the potential buyer?

With Discovery, Bob is dealing with a situation in which he does not have all the necessary elements at his disposition to take good decisions. He is missing critical information, it might be how the market is reacting is for the moment, any aspect related to the sale he did not consider yet, or simply that he does not know how to value correctly his house.

Disease as what to do advises him to look at what does not seem in good order in the house. It might be decoration, problems with plumbing, etc. Whatever it is that does not feel right should be corrected.

Beauty in what not to do, advices him to not spend too much time in the cosmetics aspects of the house.

Taken together with Disease, it would indicate that the problem is not cosmetics, but rather some things not functioning properly. As a result, he should spend more time and resources trying to fix what is broken or not working as expected.

With Discovery as the first card, we could also advise him to look more at how the housing market is. Probably getting external help, for instance a realtor, could help him to see what he is missing and remove all the uncertainties.

The French Cross

It is almost impossible to talk about French cartomancy or tarot without mentioning the ever present "tirage en croix", or French Cross, by far the most widely used spread by French speaking cartomantes.

This spread was invented by the Swiss occultist Oswald Wirth. It is described in great detail in his 1927 book, "Le Tarot des Imagiers du Moyen-Age".

It has since been a cornerstone of the French cartomancy world, to the point that it is very difficult to find any esoteric book written in French not mentioning it. It is not only used with the tarot, but also with all sorts of cartomancy systems and certainly prominent with the oracle Belline.

Over the years, a lot of authors have written about this particular spread, often coming up with their own version, which in some cases might be quite different form the original, to the point of being barely recognizable.

As a general rule, when no timeframe has been set by specific events, you can consider that a French Cross is valid up to 12 to 18 months. There is really no need to do another spread on the same subject sooner, as long as nothing changed in the querent's life as regards to their question.

The Classic French Cross

The version I describe first in this book is as close as possible to the original, and is done with 5 cards.

- Position 1 represents the querent facing their question. It will show all the assets the querent has at their disposition, what is favorable to their situation, and what can help them to move forward in the best possible way. This might be actions they take, or what others can do to help them moving forward, or any circumstances playing in their favor. Whatever it is, this position will always reveal some positive aspects of the situation.

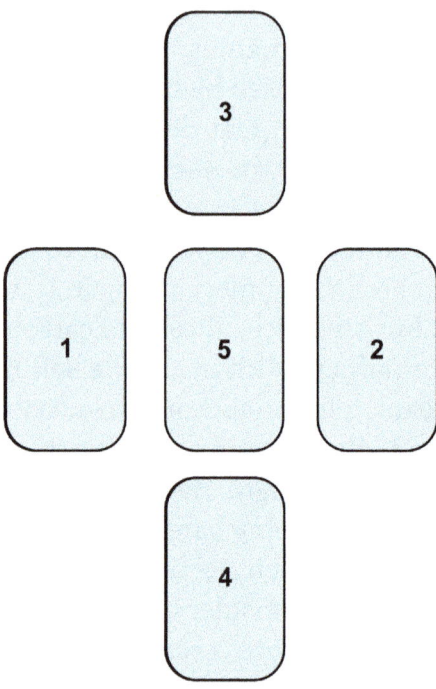

- Position 2 represents what is unfavorable, the kind of difficulties or setbacks the querent is facing. It might be some action that the querent is undertaking, or other people involved acting against the querent, or any circumstances developing against what the querent is trying to accomplish. Whatever it is, this position will always reveal what is working against what the querent wants to accomplish.
- Position 3 shows what is happening in the extended present, which can be determined as the present moment and the very near future. Depending on the

question, it might be how the situation of the querent is starting to evolve, or what advice could be given to the querent in order to move forward with their concerns in the best possible way. While positions (1) and (2) showed the favorable and unfavorable aspects of the situation the querent is facing, position (3) can be seen as how it will evolve, together with what would be the best course of action to take.
- Position 4 represents the final outcome, the result of what the querent was asking about. It can be seen as what follows the extended present, how it will develop with time, and what it will finally become. It is always interesting to compare positions (3) and (4), as it will show not only how the situation evolves, but also if we can see an improvement or a degradation.
- Position 5 is the synthesis. It can be interpreted in two different ways. First it can describe the attitude of the querent facing their question, giving an indication of how they feel concerning their problem. Second, as the synthesis links all the other positions together, it can be seen as a long term result of what is going on: is the querent going to be happy or not. As such, it becomes the long term consequences of the outcome on the querent.

Variations on the Timeline

When dealing with a situation having a very short timeline, like for instance when the result of your question is immediate or very soon, positions (3) and (4) can be changed to respectively represent the past and the extended present.

A typical use of this variation would be, for example, asking what you can do right now in regards to an already existing situation. You would respectively see in the spread the positive and negative aspects, what was already done, and what can be done now.

Will John get a promotion?

John is working in high tech and was promised a promotion to manager a while ago. He is asking about his chances to get it.

With Thought-Friendship as what is working in his favor, John is certainly seen as someone who is welcoming and can easily establish new friendships with others. He is certainly appreciated, a quality that can help him to get support later and have people he can rely on to further his goals of being promoted.

Union as what is working against him shows that John is not always a team player. There might be difficulties in establishing common goals for the team, or a strategy to reach them. This card shows some discord or dysfunction in how John's team works, and his commitment might be put into question.

It might be troubling to find these two cards opposed to each other, what are the positive and negative aspects to the situation. If we try to navigate this conflict, one of the cards is about relation with others, while the other is about commitments. This shows clearly a picture where we can see that John can easily establish contacts with others and have a friendly attitude. But at the same time, his commitment to his team or projects is put into question. We could say that he has the human qualities needed to lead and become a manager, but his is lacking reliability when it comes to what the company wants.

If we look at the extended present, with Peace, the atmosphere is quiet and not much is happening. There is kind of a tacit agreement where things remain calm and waiting to see what will happen over time. At the same time, as we have seen with the first two cards, there is a latent conflict between the two attitudes that could easily impact the current situation. As a result, keeping the peace might not be easy and John is advised to keep a low profile and try to compromise for the future.

This is directly leading to Discovery, he is not ready right now for his promotion, there are things that he has to be aware of first, and certainly a development plan on how to proceed forward is necessary, in order for him to remedy the problems we saw earlier.

Gifts, at outcome, shows that the actions hinted in Discovery will be successful, John will get the promotion, but later than expected, after completion of the development plan.

If we look at the planets to grab some more information, two cards under the influence of the Sun show that success is absolutely possible, especially with one of them as outcome. Two cards influenced by Venus show how important relations with others are. And finally one card related to the Moon shows how the situation is uncertain to start with, and that he will have to solve some things that were unclear.

Is Sally going to find happiness?
Sally is 37, married for twelve years with two children. Having marital problems, she just met someone else at work and is asking how their relation will progress.

It might feel strange to get a card such as Betrayal in what is favorable for Sally, but let's not forget the question, which is about having an extramarital affair. And in this case, the first card is just highlighting the fact that her marriage is facing difficulties and that in that case, testing the waters outside of her marriage could represent a favorable experience for Sally. She should effectively think about herself first and hide from her husband what is going on.

Gifts in position 2 is more problematic, as the card hints that she will not get much support and it will not be easy for her to see her lover. Effectively, she can count only on herself, and maybe he is less committed than she thinks, he might not be ready to move their relationship to something more serious.

With Change as the extended present, we see a period of uncertainty, where trying to find stability for the relationship is not possible. As hinted before, with Gifts as the unfavorable aspect, there might be reluctance to move that opportunity forward and having a positive evolution for the hidden relationship.

As the synthesis is showing with Fire, what is happening with her lover was first about satisfying primal needs, not really about love but rather a fire burning between them because of physical attraction. It became intense, but with the surrounding cards there is nothing to sustain that fire. As Change was hinting at, it will not last, the relationship will not become stable enough to be sustained, and the Penates as outcome shows a return to her home life and family. It seems that the fire found in the synthesis will be extinguished rapidly.

The two cards influenced by the Moon show so much uncertainties that it is probably not a good idea for her to take the next step with her lover, especially with one of these moon cards as the outcome. But when looking at a reading, it is often as important to pay attention to what is not there, sometimes as much as what is present. And what we see in this reading is than no card is under the influence of Venus, which would show true feelings or love. This is confirming the Mars energy we find as synthesis, high energy but that does not last.

An Extended Version

There are two areas which can cause some confusion when doing a classic French Cross. My experience, having dealt with this spread for many years and done thousands of readings, showed me that two areas needed some improvement.

First, it always seems that the most difficult position to understand correctly is position (2), what is unfavorable. While it is always easy to understand the forces playing in your favor, it is often more difficult to exactly determine what the problem can be. This makes perfect sense, as most of the time we know very well our strengths, but have difficulties to define correctly our defaults. This is certainly part of human nature.

In the diagram, position (6) helps alleviating this problem. It represents the forces and attitudes describing position (2). It does not change the meanings of position (2), what is problematic for the querent. It explains why they're having the problems or how it can be better defined. Please refer to the examples below to see how we can benefit from this additional card.

Second, I never liked the duality expressed by the

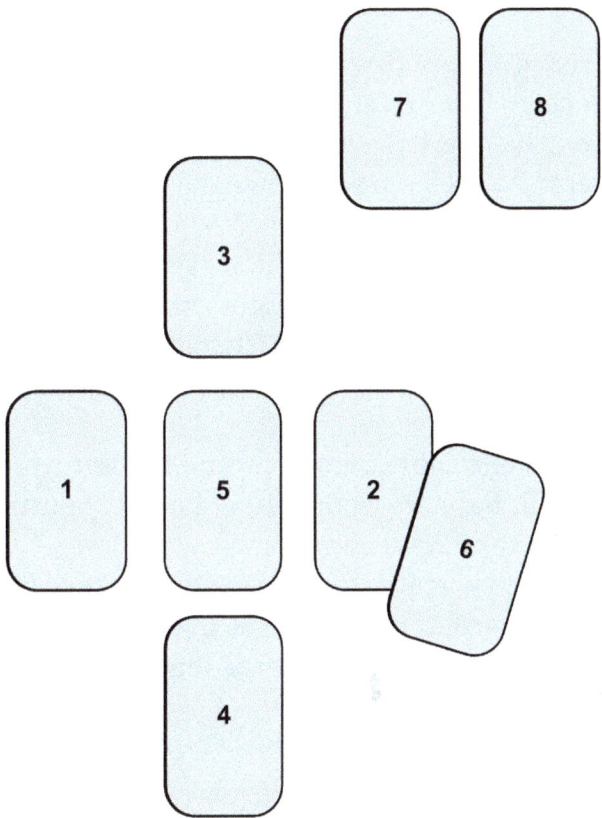

synthesis, which can be at the same time the mood of the querent facing their question, and the long term consequences.

As a result, in the way I read a French Cross, I always start with position (5), the synthesis, and interpret it as what are the feelings the querent has in regards to their question, what is their attitude. This is very important as the way they look at things is going to heavily influence their behavior. A querent having a very positive attitude is going to minimize the problems, while a very pessimistic one is going to emphasize the problems. Knowing how they feel will greatly help you to navigate the spread and focus their attention on some parts.

Positions (7) and (8) are what I call the long term consequences. They explain what will be the result of the outcome on the querent's life and their consequences over the long term. As such, these become the logical following to position (4).

For instance, the querent might not get the job they really wanted, but long term they might see that some other opportunity would be better for them, or that travel and commuting are becoming too much and impacting their relationship.

Or their lover might come back, and the same problems as before will happen again after a while, putting the querent in a very difficult situation.

I like to draw two cards for this position instead of one, as it has a very important impact on the querent's life. I usually mix the definitions of the two cards together to come to a conclusion.

Let's go back to the two previous examples.

John's promotion

Fame in position 6 explains very well why John will not receive his promotion in the near future, he does not have enough recognition from his peers. As we have seen, he is not really a team player and his lack of commitment to his team is hurting his chances. As a result, some people surrounding him and his managers do not feel that he is not reliable enough to get responsibilities, he has not gained enough support.

The French Cross

Looking at the long term, something is going to hold him back. Even if he gets promoted, as we've seen, the fact that he was put on a development plan was certainly a bad sign, and will have consequences on any eventual future development of his career.

Delay followed by Enterprises show that he cannot come to a complete realization of his ambitions. Even if Enterprises show that his career is evolving, that evolution will be slower than he expects. He is going to be blocked from any other promotion for a long time.

Sally's marital situation

As we did with the previous example, we will not review the whole reading, but just add what is revealed by the extra cards.

Looking at position (6), we get Misfortune. So, even if it was in her advantage to test the waters outside of her marriage as Betrayal was indicating, she certainly has feelings of guilt doing it. She feels that the situation could take a bad turn and leave her in a very unfortunate situation. As we have seen with Gifts and the lack of support she is getting, she might become completely demoralized, and find difficult to leave her marriage, feeling that this adventure would not give her anything of value compared to what she already has.

Long term, she will use her judgement, and with time passing she will understand much better what happened and what were her motivations at that time. This will allow her to appreciate environment, marriage and children better. As we have seen earlier, Fire as synthesis was showing that what happened was just a moment of passion that did not last.

The Snapshot Spread

The Snapshot is a spread that I use at the beginning of a consultation when there is no specific question, or when someone desires a general reading. It allows me to quickly diagnose what is happening in the life of the querent at the time of the consultation.

As some consultants do not want to ask a question, or desire a general reading, we cannot start by using a specific spread like the French Cross, for instance, we need something more generic. It would be possible to use a spread such a the Astrological Spread, sometimes called the Horoscope Spread, or any other general purpose spread. But in my experience, I don't like to use these too much as they tend to stay general in nature instead of going deeply into specific issues.

In such cases, I will use the Snapshot Spread as it allows to quickly determine what is going on in the querent's life and what areas of their life needs some attention. When this is done, we can then use other specialized spreads such as the French Cross or the Advice Spread to dig into the areas showing signs of problems and give a deeper and more appropriate reading.

The Snapshot Spread is made of 11 cards, positioned in the form of a pyramid, and is straightforward to use. It is made of 3 rows: the top one represents the attitudes of the querent, the second one the material aspects in their life, and the third one deals with relations and emotional aspects.

- Position 1 is the synthesis. It will show the mood of the querent at the moment of the consultation, what their attitude is facing their problems and their life in general. A very important position, as the card drawn here will have some influence on all the others.

The Snapshot Spread

- Positions 2 and 3 will show what is happening with their work. This can also include hobbies and other activities the querent takes part in.
- Positions 4 and 5 will deal with money and possessions.
- Positions 6 and 7 are about relationships and love interests in general.
- Positions 8 and 9 will describe their spiritual life, how they feel on a psychological level.
- Positions 10 and 11 will deal with the querent's social life, their relations with friends, family, and at large.

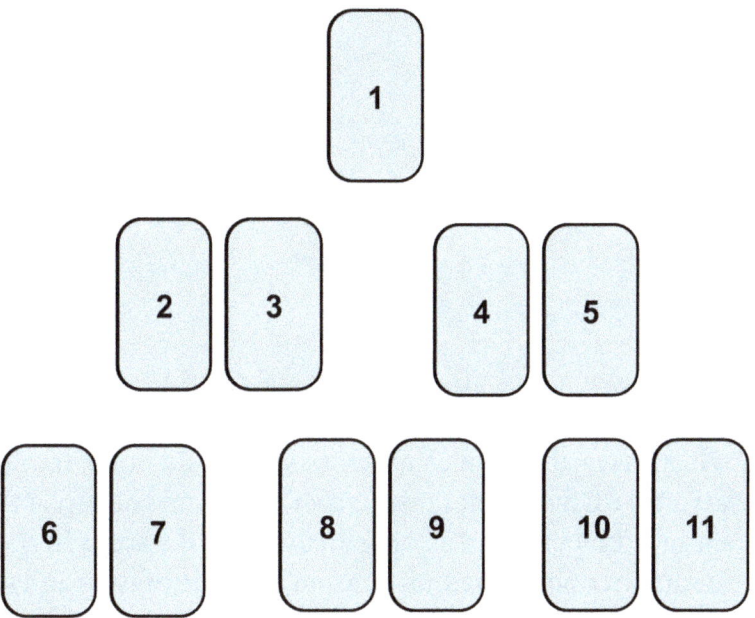

What is important in interpreting the pairs is to blend the two cards together, and also to take into account the card in position 1 as influence.

The case of Olivia

Olivia is in her 40s and single. Let's look at what the energies were around her when she came for a consultation.

Let's have a look first at her state of mind. With Delay, Olivia can expect some setbacks or some of her actions not moving forward, or not as much as she would hope. It might be also that Olivia is her own worst enemy in the sense that she might be pessimistic, or reluctant to take steps in order to further her objectives. She has an attitude of wait and see, not ready to take any risk.

For work, positions 2 and 3, her projects are evolving in the right direction. Destiny would hint at something important happening, and with Enterprises, there might be a possibility of a new job or something new in her current activity. Whatever it is, the work situation is great, she is

The Snapshot Spread

ready for new adventures which will become key for her.

Moneywise, positions 4 and 5, her current situation is not as easy. Misfortune shows a lack of financial resources, she has put herself in a dire situation, one where some action should be taken, for instance to repair her credit or pay back some debts or credit cards. Whatever it is Countryside-Health suggests to cool down on the spending.

At this point it is interesting to consider for a moment the complete line, as usually the job and financial situation are linked, as often the money we get comes form our work. And here Misfortune, coupled with Enterprises could certainly hint at Enterprises showing the necessity for her to find a new job that could improve her financial situation. This has become very important for her.

Positions 6 and 7 are about her love interests, and let's not forget that Olivia is not in a committed relationship. With Fire Olivia should not expect something very stable in the relationship department, but more of an atmosphere leading to dating, or a few adventures. Something that quickly ignites a fire but does not last and might become quickly conflictual. Intelligence is balancing very well the energies of Fire as she is capable of taking a step back and understand what is going on. She will quickly see things for what they are.

This might be due to what we see in the remaining of the line. For her social line, we see difficult dealings. She has to deal with difficult people, and Enemies shows some venom sometimes exchanged with others.

This might also explain why we have Meanness and Penates for how she feels psychologically. As she feels all that opposition and a sense of toxicity around her, she is someone who retreats easily and closes herself to others.

This third line might also explain in part why we get

Delay on top, she has certainly developed an attitude of mistrust in regards to others.

Now we understand better what is going on with Olivia. We might continue with a reading on how her job hunt is going to evolve, and another one on her social life. These two aspects seem to be the highest priority. As we have seen earlier, the social aspect is certainly impacting her love life, and as a result should be dealt with first. When this first step is complete, other readings could be done. Depending on how evolves the job hunt, we could look at the evolution of her finances. Same with relationships, as they certainly depend on her social interactions.

One Question, One Card

An alternative to spreads is to use the technique of successively asking simple questions, and pulling one card for responding to each one, continuing until all the necessary information has been obtained.

This technique could be used for instance when the usual spreads do not seem fit for the question you are asking, or in complement to a standard spread when more information is needed. As long as the questions remain simple, as explained in the guidelines at the beginning of this chapter, this is a great way to look at a particular problem. This system also allows you to gain a lot of flexibility, adapting your questions to what has already been answered.

Let's take a practical example. Jane is responsible for the sales department in a company and needs to hire a new member for her team. Dan seems to be the ideal candidate, and Jane comes to us to do a reading about Dan and how he would fit in her organization.

In a case like this, even before looking at how Dan would evolve in the company, we could start by asking a few simple questions to get an idea about the kind of person he is. Once we have dressed his psychological profile, we will be able to decide what to ask next.

We could start, for instance, by asking what kind of  person Dan is. The question seems relevant, as we want to know how he would integrate with the team. The card pulled is Elevation (6). Right away, we could say that Dan is someone who easily gains perspective when faced with any situation. He can see how everything fits from a global point of view, a good quality which would allow him to concentrate on the whole issues he would be facing instead of being too detail-oriented. This is also someone who could take the next step and be on the path to more responsibilities or management some day.

Now, let's see how he would act with his customers. We get Changes (18). Let's not forget when interpreting this card, that we still have to take into account the previous card, as it was describing Dan in general. So, the main traits of characters we saw, leadership, gaining perspective, etc. will remain, but tainted by Changes when dealing with customers.

So, we have a card under the influence of Mercury, describing him as a good communicator, someone who would have a good relationship with his customers. Changes would also show that it is easy for him to adapt to many different situations, he is flexible in his approach to problems. Just a small concern, Changes could now indicate someone who would be easily swayed by the customer's reactions.

Let's look also at how Dan would fit with the team, how he would be with his colleagues. The card drawn is Peace (26). Being someone with a tendency to bury the hatchet easily, we can see Dan as someone who tries to avoid conflicts and always look for a compromise, how a difficult situation could be alleviated. He is someone who is looking for a consensus first, avoiding disputes. All these qualities, taken together with what was explained with Elevation, reaffirm his qualities as a leader, and someone always looking for satisfying solutions.

Looking at all this, Dan seems to be a very promising

candidate. At this point a French Cross, for instance, to see how he would evolve with the company would be advised.

Part 4
Appendices

Keywords

1 Destiny	knowledge, discovery, decision to make, access, chance, success.
2 Man's Star	the querent or important man
3 Woman's Star	the querent or important woman
4 Nativity	beginning, birth, something starting, new project, emergence
5 Success	success, rewards, favorable outcome, victory, profit, retribution
6 Elevation	ascension, gain of altitude, global view, progression, ambition
7 Honors	recognition, acceptance, distinction, gratitude, pride, notoriety
8 Thought Friendship	altruism, fidelity, protection, benevolence, loyalty, sincerity, harmony
9 Countryside Health	vacation, leisure, relaxation, nature, tranquility, rejuvenation, serenity
10 Gifts	gratification, generosity, retribution, gain, favors, donation
11 Betrayal	deception, betrayal, lack of loyalty, infidelity, lust, lack of confidence
12 Departure	leaving behind, new projects, emancipation, freedom, renewal
13 Inconstancy	indecision, hesitation, unpredictable, versatile, movement, fluctuation, superficial
14 Discovery	exploration, learning something new, knowledge, understanding
15 Water	moodiness, emotions, journey, travel, intuition, anxieties
16 Penates	home, security, building, shelter, safe place, family
17 Disease	dysfunction, inconvenience, trouble, imbalance, displeasure
18 Change	modification, transformation, evolution, mutation
19 Money	abundance, enrichment, opulence, profusion, wealth, financial success

20 Intelligence	understanding, knowledge, discovering, adaptability, comprehension
21 Theft - Loss	fear, loss, material worry, breach of trust, negligence, waste of time or resources
22 Enterprises	project, undertake, plan, skills, conception, tools
23 Traffic	travel, exchanges, negotiation, meetings, sales and purchases
24 News	message, mail, surprise, visit, changes, unexpected events
25 Pleasures	joy, contentment, bliss, amusement, being artistic, artistic pleasure
26 Peace	reconciliation, agreement, appeasement, tranquility
27 Union	commitment, love, marriage, promise, availability
28 Family	family, close friendship, trusted association, group, shared interests
29 Love	love, happiness, feelings, pleasure, relationship
30 The Table	conviviality, pleasure, entertainment, sharing, celebration
31 Passions	ardor, irrational love, desire, attraction
32 Meanness	selfishness, cruelty, vice, unkindness, treason
33 Trial	conflict, opposition, antagonism, dispute, debate
34 Despotism	authority, inability to act, submission, resignation, passivity
35 Enemies	hostility, malevolence, significant difficulties, adversity, competition, malice
36 Negotiations	discussions, debate, exchange, diplomacy, gossip
37 Fire	dynamism, drive, determination, strength, will, fight
38 Accident	unforeseen events, change, unexpected modification, collapse, destruction
39 Support	help, assistance, support, solid foundations, kindness
40 Beauty	aesthetics, flourish, harmony, luxury, sensitivity, arts

41 Heritage	transmission, acquired wisdom, experience, relating to the past, succession, inheritance
42 Wisdom	intelligence, maturity, serenity, mastery, life experience
43 Fame	popularity, notoriety, celebrity, reputation, recognition
44 Hazard	unforeseen events, opportunities, movement, luck, dynamism
45 Happiness	joy, success, pleasure, conviviality, wealth
46 Misfortune	difficulties, handicap, bad luck, unfortunate events, problematic situation
47 Sterility	barren, unproductive, infertile, incapacity, stalemate
48 Fatality	deadline, test of time, destiny, fate, transformation (often inevitable
49 Grace	blessing, generosity, spiritual protection, favor, absolution
50 Ruin	old, old fashioned, outdated, collapse, destruction, debacle
51 Delay	slowness, waiting, setback, slowdown, unforeseen event
52 Cloister	isolation, loneliness, renunciation, monastery, grid, fence

Marcel Forget, aka Belline

There is not much information available about Belline. Most of what I relate in this appendix comes from an interview he gave to Jacques Chancel's Radioscopie radio show on September 29th, 1972, and from what he relates in the three books he wrote in French, "Un Voyant à la Recherché du Temps Futur", "Anthologies de l'Au-delà", and "La Troisième Oreille".

Belline, who was one of the greatest clairvoyants of the twentieth century, was nicknamed "the prince of psychics".

Born Marcel Forget in 1924, the son of a bourgeois family, he was in his youth passionate about history and antiques, and was predestined to become an arts and antique dealer. He had a lot of sensitivity for all the arts, and antiques fascinated him.

Being also a fervent admirer of old books, he was buying old treatises, among other things, esotericism and spiritualism. That's how he found in an old attic a book written by Jean des Vignes Rouges, "an essay on modern chiromancy". Intrigued, Belline dives in and develops an insatiable curiosity for all sorts of divinatory arts.

That's how he learned numerology, astrology and even some tarotmancy. But his real gift became palmistry, he had a read gift for reading the lines of a hand.

During the second world war, Belline became sick and was admitted to a sanatorium. That's where he started to have visions. One day, he started having violent stomach aches that had nothing to do with his own ailments. His intuition made him realize that these sufferings concerned his neighbor, who was physically in another room. He had no physical contact with him. Calling the medical staff, he convinced them to check on the neighbor who was found to suffer from an intestinal occlusion. The patient's condition confirmed the accurate prediction of Belline.

Following this episode, a lot of patients consulted him and that's how he started to discover his gifts and develop them. However, it was not until the mid-1950s that he finally completely accepted being the recipient of such gifts, and opened a psychic practice, at 45 Rue Fontaine in Paris, the same street where the Mage Edmond was practicing a century earlier. That's apparently when he started to call himself Belline. He practiced in this place until the mid-1980s.

A few newspapers started reporting his predictions that proved to be correct, making him famous. Among other things, he predicted that Eisenhower would suffer from a heart attack, which happened three months later. This was the prediction that really started his period of fame. He also predicted the polio vaccine, Einstein's death, the suicide of Marilyn Monroe, the riots associated with May '68, and many other events.

He was always honest with his clients, never lying to them. If nothing came to him, he simply told the querent that no information was coming. That's how one day an older woman came to consult him, and he apologized because he had nothing to tell her. Surprised by so much honesty, and knowing his passion for art and antiques, she invited him to her place, telling him that she had in her attic old papers he might be interested in.

Belline didn't visit her quickly enough and a few days later the woman called him to explain that if he was not coming quickly, she would burn these old papers the next day. Belline hurried to visit her and that's how he discovered old parchments and two beautiful card games. These dated from the previous century and were the work of Jules Charles Ernest Billaudot, nicknamed Mage Edmond. These card games are the ones known today as the Oracle Belline and the Grand Tarot Belline. Belline used his influence to get them published a soon as possible.

The Mage Edmond, a century earlier, practiced in the same street as Belline, at 30 Rue Fontaine. Not much information is available on his life. He was born on August 17th 1829 in the small city of Poilly sur Serein, in the French department of Yonne, and died May 20th 1881, in La Chapelle-Vielle-Forêt. He was apparently famous for the predictions he gave to Alexandre Dumas, Auguste Renoir, and the emperor Napoléon III, among others.

Later in life, Belline was very afflicted by a personal tragedy. He lost his son in a car accident in August 1969. In his book, "La Troisième Oreille", he explains how he woke up during the night with the premonition of his son dying. He was not surprised to be made aware of the circumstances when the police came to his door at 6AM. His son never regained consciousness and died three days later. He relates in his book all the dialogs he has with his son through mediumship.

Belline continued his psychic practice until the mid-1980s, when he faded out completely of the public eye. There is even some discrepancy on when he died, with some sources mentioning 1994, while his editor gives the date of 2002.

Acknowledgements

First and foremost, I thank my wife Catherine and her sister Michelle. Without them, I would never have discovered the wonderful world of the cards and divination.

I owe much to Alison Cross, who proofread this manuscript and gave me so much good advice.

This book would not exist without Maria Alviz Hernando and the wonderful group on the oracle Belline she leads at the World Divination Association. Without them I would never have had the idea of writing a guide on this oracle.

A special mention to Lisa Young-Sutton, who was always available when I needed advice on self-publishing.

Last and not least, a big thank you to all the divination students I had over the years. Teaching is a wonderful activity, where you learn as much as you teach. It gave me the discipline to structure to my ideas and to express them in a formal way, two essential qualities for writing a book.

www.ingramcontent.com/pod-product-compliance
Lightning Source LLC
Chambersburg PA
CBHW050859160426
43194CB00011B/2215